THE PATH OF THE
MOONLIGHT

The memoirs of a sailor's wife

KATHLEEN LOCKE

WITH NOTES BY HER DAUGHTER, SHELAGH BELL

MEREO
Cirencester

LYM

Mereo Books

1A The Wool Market Dyer Street Cirencester Gloucestershire GL7 2PR
An imprint of Memoirs Publishing www.mereobooks.com

The Path of the Moonlight: 978-1-86151-499-8

First published in Great Britain in 2015
by Mereo Books, an imprint of Memoirs Publishing

The address for Memoirs Publishing Group Limited can be found at
www.memoirspublishing.com

The Memoirs Publishing Group Ltd Reg. No. 7834348

The Memoirs Publishing Group supports both The Forest Stewardship Council® (FSC®) and
the PEFC® leading international forest-certification organisations. Our books carrying both the
FSC label and the PEFC® and are printed on FSC®-certified paper. FSC® is the only
forest-certification scheme supported by the leading environmental organisations including
Greenpeace. Our paper procurement policy can be found at
www.memoirspublishing.com/environment

Typeset in 12/18pt Bembo
by Wiltshire Associates Publisher Services Ltd. Printed and bound in Great Britain by
Printondemand-Worldwide, Peterborough PE2 6XD

To the late John Locke and his
wife 'Bunny', both sadly missed.

CONTENTS

Foreword

FOREWORD

While sorting out my mother's things after she moved into a nursing home, I came across a pile of untidy pages, very badly typed, none in order, some re-typed and a lot of crossings-out. Some had been screwed up and then straightened out again. It took me quite some time to sort them all out. They were the memoirs she had once mentioned to me that she was writing, a comment not taken very seriously at the time as it was assumed it would be a few jottings she would soon get tired of.

She had bought a very old, almost clapped-out typewriter from an auction sale and being no typist herself, she had painfully tapped out her story using one finger. It was quite an achievement for someone in her eighties. Her memory was then very good and I think she hoped to record her experiences before old age took its toll and they inevitably faded into a forgotten past. My late brother had originally printed them out in booklet form for family interest, but I am now hoping they might reach a wider public and perhaps stir a few memories of old times. The notes in the first part were to correct one or two inaccuracies and explain a little more about family members which, I realise, would not be terribly interesting to the general public, but I have included them just the same and hope no one will get too bored.

Reading through her memoirs, I could not help but be amused by her obsession with the constant house-hunting and the excuses she always came up with for it. It was a bit of a joke in the family. Her earliest reminiscences were of course gleaned from hearsay, probably from her own mother, who also liked to talk of old times, and if they probably sound a bit egocentric, read on, they get better!

My mother's observations could be taken as part of 20th century history with its two world wars and the lives of most middle-class women, who were not expected to work for a living, with marriage their only career. She was no feminist and never questioned that arrangement, but she was intelligent and perhaps unconsciously irked by such narrow confines. Her other obsessions after house-hunting, were cats and contract bridge. Cats came second in her affections after my father, children a poor third. She was an expert needlewoman. I was the next generation to be recruited to the empire of the tireless and ageless Misses Bird and a somewhat reluctant recruit to their many dancing concerts, once so well-known in Southampton, but now only a memory to the older residents. My mother made all my costumes, including one she did when I was given the part of a butterfly at the age of about four. A rather clumsy one, as in my enthusiasm to fly, I nearly fell off the stage!

She idolised my father and his death probably affected her more than most of us realised. They had both depended to a large extent on each other and when he died, she lost all her previous interest in house-hunting. She continued to live at Lyme Regis with my brother John and his family and might have been content with that arrangement to the end of her days, until John was promoted in his naval career and given a shore job in Portsmouth, so the house at Lyme Regis had to be given up. My father's pension died with him and Mum was left virtually penniless. Neither of them had ever been good with money, although he might have curbed her spendthrift ways had he been in better health. As a captain in the Cunard Line of the 50s and 60s, his salary was never very high. It used to be a standard joke in Southampton that when a ship docked, the stewards were met by their wives in Bentleys and Rolls Royces, while the captain, carrying his bundle of dirty washing, went home by tram. There was a lot of truth in that!

After my father's death, to make ends meet, my mother found herself a job (for the first time in her life) as companion to an elderly lady living some distance away. It did not work out and after a few weeks, she left and returned to Lyme Regis. The cats, she discovered, had run away soon after being rehomed.. She scoured the countryside for them and after a long search, eventually found them wandering, starving and near death. Sadly, they had to be put down. There were no more cats after that.

When John and his family moved to Portsmouth, Mum returned to Lymington, where her younger brother, Mervyn, found her a privately-owned sheltered housing scheme. Later, the owner decided to sell the whole site, and for once, she dug in her heels and refused to move. But she was obliged to do so in the end, and went to council-owned sheltered accommodation a mile or two away. John, although he could ill-afford it with his large family, continued to help her with money, while the rest of us, I am ashamed to say, were not as generous. However, she finished up in a beautiful charity-run nursing home in Farnborough, where she died at the age of 94.

I am grateful for her memoirs. I wish I had been kinder to her. They give an insight into her character and the times she lived in. As a daughter who did not always see eye to eye with her, I can now feel some sympathy and understanding with her. What did surprise me in her account was the fact that, in spite of repeated attacks of pneumonia and emphysema lasting over many years, and a lifetime's history of smoking, the true nature of my father's illness was only discovered about two days before he died. The dangers of tobacco were only just being realised.

Shelagh Bell

CHAPTER ONE

UNE ENFANT TERRIBLE

It was on April 18ᵗʰ 1900, at number 26 Carlton Crescent, Southampton, that the 'monthly nurse' and our family doctor flanked my mother's big double bed, exhorting her from time to time to be brave, to pull on the towel fixed to the brass rails at the end of the bed and to 'keep pushing dear and it will soon be over'. Waves of ever-increasing pain threatened to submerge my poor mother into the depths of despair and misery (it was her first baby and she was quite convinced she was utterly done for). She uttered scream after scream, greatly alarming my father, who was pacing the dining room below. He longed to rush upstairs and find out what was going on, but dared not enter the hallowed torture chamber until the summons had come from those in charge of proceedings.

But as is usually the case, everything quietened down and the only sound emanating from behind that door was a thin wail. Within minutes, a smiling doctor emerged, slowly descended the stairs and informed my harassed father that I had arrived.

To the disgust and contempt of the nurse, my mother was unable to feed me herself. As there were few suitable baby foods on the market the consequence was that I howled morning and night with hunger and looked set to continue the protest. Nurse never ceased to reiterate that there was nothing to equal mother's milk (as if the mother in question was deliberately withholding her bounty). No one indeed disputed her argument as to the efficacy of Nature's provision, but in its absence, what to do about it?

After about a week, to everyone's relief, Nurse took herself off and the same afternoon, a young and trusted nanny arrived to take her place.

Her name was Nurse Spray and from the moment she set foot inside our house, kissed her distraught mistress and took her first look at me, her miserable, skinny charge, the atmosphere seemed to lighten. Nanny Spray dumped her bags in the hallway, her self-confidence communicating itself to all present. She took me gently from my mother's arms and given the location, straight away carried me upstairs to the nursery. She knew what to do. She had the special formula for feeding babies and there was peace from then on.

Once she was established as part of the household, her hands were never idle. Nothing was too much trouble and if at times, both mind and body must have ached with fatigue, no one ever knew. She considered time was too precious to give way to mere tiredness. Nothing, in her opinion, could justify shelving responsibilities except illness or death, and she said she had no intention of giving way to either.

So in this extremely favourable atmosphere I soon made up for lost time, becoming daily healthier and less skinny, transformed from an unprepossessing infant into a reasonably pleasant child.

Of course my parents were delighted. Now they could enjoy all the pleasures of motherhood and fatherhood with none of the work and worry. They joined with Nanny Spray in rejoicing over my almost uninterrupted progress, showing their gratitude in ways she was often quite reluctant to accept. She remarked that after all, it was only her duty and the happy results of her ministrations were in themselves sufficient recompense, without any other reward.

We were lucky also in having good and trustworthy maids to run the house, which had twenty rooms, and they all agreed to come with us when, a year or two later, we moved into another large Victorian house further down the street.

My father was a hard-working solicitor and an active member of innumerable clubs and committees. He subscribed to the axiom 'to know all is to forgive all', and practised this forgiveness to the extent of overlooking some bad debts on the part of certain clients. This did not altogether meet with approval as far as my mother was concerned. She never knew exactly what he earned – few wives did then – but saw no reason why, with a family to provide for, he should work 'for love'.

★Note: One did not need to be particularly well-off to afford domestic staff in the late-Victorian period. It was virtually the only career open to a working-class girl and labour was plentiful. Some treated their staff well and even regarded them as part of the family, while some were poorly-paid skivvies to the end of their days. From what I can tell, the Blatches of the time were among the former. I do hope so. Nurse Spray's word was law and she virtually ruled the household. In the 1901 census, Emily Jane Spray, born Exeter 1873, was described in the census as "a certificated hospital nurse".

At the age of three months, dressed in a lace-trimmed embroidered and tucked robe and in the company of numerous relations and friends of my parents, I was christened at St Mary's (Southampton's mother church, then without its tall spire). Following the ceremony there was a party at which a large number of those rather uninteresting gifts considered suitable for christenings were presented, mostly of silver and therefore of intrinsic value to be stored away before, very many years later, turning up at auction sales. A huge tea was laid in the garden with lots of white lace tablecloths, ornate silver teapots and delicate, elegant china. Everyone enjoyed the sandwiches and home-made cakes. That is, everyone except the central figure, who went to sleep, and my mother, who without fail, as was her wont, developed the usual migraine and by the end of the afternoon was confined to her bed in a darkened room.

She was quite a pretty woman, although never a match to her husband in intellect, and had a serene expression. She could sometimes even look beautiful despite wearing no make-up, rather unbecoming clothes (as clothes were in those days) and a heavy hairstyle. But with a loving family, good health, no money worries and a loyal and willing staff, to say nothing of her devoted and indispensable nanny, she could not be anything but happy. And she was.

Unfortunately for her, she had a sociable husband who loved entertaining. It was the one drawback of her otherwise idyllic existence. Her inherent shyness and frequent migraine headaches, often occurring at inopportune times when she had to meet new and occasionally (so she thought) awe-inspiring people, were distinct disadvantages. But my father adored her and she him. A more devoted couple there probably never was.

The law so often conjures up a picture of stuffy pomposity. At the time in partnership with his brother, my father was in no way a prototype of such rigid characterisation. A kind man, with a good sense of humour and a tremendous zest for life, he had many and diverse interests. In some respects, he probably worked too hard, with much of his time devoted to lost causes and sometimes lost cases.

One lost cause, if not a lost case, concerned a local builder, one of my father's clients, who was often at loggerheads with the Council on some infringement or other of the local bye-laws. Constantly refusing to take professional advice, he may even have enjoyed his tussle with the local bureaucrats. One day my father managed to get him off having to pay a large fine on the basis of a legal technicality. No sooner had they both returned to their respective homes than the builder, in a frenzy of excitement after his triumph over the Council, rang up and started one of his usual interminable conversations. Lunch had just arrived on the table of the Blatch establishment and was rapidly cooling while my father, courteous as ever, endured the torrent of words. But the caller's victory proved short-lived and sadly, so did he. A severe stroke, brought on by all the undue agitation, killed him that same day.

Friendly with everyone, even with the most antagonistic of Council members (and there were inevitably a few, some opposed politically), my father himself later joined the Council and later still, while at the same time serving on numerous committees and giving himself far too much to do, he became one of Southampton's most popular sheriffs and mayors. He loved music and in spite of having little leisure time he composed the score of several charming operettas for a great friend who was the local scoutmaster, a Doctor Emlyn. Every so often these operettas, published by Curwen and Co., were performed in public by the scout troop who, it is to be hoped, enjoyed rendering the melodies as much as Father enjoyed composing them.

He was a JP and a member of the Rotary Club, for whose dinners he rehearsed long and I thought rather boring speeches (this was probably because my mother and I had to be practice audiences). He was also a member of the Health Committee and active in the Hampshire Field Club and the Hampshire County Cricket Club, whose matches he rarely missed, particularly when they played Kent. Although quick-tempered, he never bore a grudge and always liked to hear the other fellow's point of view. Altogether, he was a kind and loving husband and loyal working colleague.

Uncle Ben, grim and unsmiling, was the personification of the stuffy, pompous lawyer and a keen adherent to the maxim that children should be seen and not heard. When I was old enough to join my parents at lunch, he often threatened to cut off my hands if I put my elbows on the table and despite Nanny's reassurances, I fully believed him. Needless to say, I was scared stiff of him. The founder of the family firm was, I understand, a great uncle called Thomas Goater. When my father worked there, the senior partner of the business was a T. Goater whose offices were at Number 10, Portland Terrace, a tall, narrow building near the High Street. Goater, as I remember him, was a fairly typical Dickensian lawyer, slow and ponderous in all dealings with clients, with a maddening 'this year, next year' attitude toward any case under his jurisdiction. Father, on the other hand, liked to get on with things, to clear his desk of the inevitable pile of office papers, letters, pamphlets and heavy, dusty law books that cluttered his colleague's massive mahogany desk, to such an extent that he could never lay his hands on any particular document when it was needed. When Benjamin later joined the firm as a fully-fledged partner, things were, if anything, worse. He would not allow anything to be moved or even dusted, and woe betide any maidservant who tried to remove the top layer.

My father liked to arrange dinner parties from time to time for clients and business acquaintances. My mother was usually struck by the inevitable migraine on these occasions, progressing in severity as the painful hours dragged by, so that by late afternoon, he had no option but to hastily summon the nearest available relative to act as hostess in her place. Genteel 'at homes' with her own friends sitting around and chatting and drinking tea she could take in her stride, but dinner parties lasting well into the small hours, never!

Although I have no actual memory of it now, the house in Carlton Crescent at Number 26 must have been very cold, despite the many fires lit daily during the winter months. Certainly the cosiest and most homely room in the whole house was the sunny nursery, and this I can recall clearly. While always keeping a wary eye on me, an increasingly active crawler and later toddler, Nanny did endless needlework and crochet, mending with the finest of stitching and making me tucked and frilly dresses – white, always white. I never wore them more than once before they were carefully hand-laundered. The carpet on the floor was thick with woolly rugs to keep out draughts, the curtains hanging from their poles by huge brass rings, and in the centre of the room was a large table covered with a red bobbled chenille cloth, handy for pulling off by exploring toddlers. The focal point was the wonderfully bright fire, sending red and gold flames leaping into the wide chimney behind the brass-bound guard.

One day, just after my second birthday, Nanny came into the nursery smiling all over her kindly face. "Do you know what the doctor has brought you?" she said. I stared blankly at her, not associating doctors with Father Christmas. She went on, pausing slightly for effect: "A new baby brother! Isn't that lovely?"

I suppose at two years old, I must have vaguely wondered if baby brothers came in various assortments, new, second-hand or well played-with, and what they were anyway. I was, of course, soon to find out.

Chapter Two

The Intruder

My new brother was named Cecil Herbert Spence, and he made up for all the desirable attributes I had lacked at birth. Nanny propelled his reluctant sister into our parents' bedroom for our first introduction to each other, but when I saw him cuddled in my mother's arms and took in the expression on her face as she gazed down at him, I felt a fierce stab of jealousy. This thing, this 'brother' had somehow or other gatecrashed into our happy home, and I disapproved strongly. Now Nanny's ample lap no longer belonged to me but mostly to this interloper.

At mealtimes, I was banished (or so it felt) to a hard chair and a little nearby table of my own where I sat gloomily shovelling spoonfuls of beef gravy and potato into my mouth (or onto the floor) while keeping a wary and resentful eye on Cecil as he happily gulped his bottle in Nanny's arms.

To make matters worse, he was such a good and lovable baby. From the first, he was healthy, chubby and fair of face, sucked contentedly at his bottle from the word 'go' and hardly ever cried. I wore a perpetual scowl on my disagreeable face and showed my intense dislike of the situation by deliberately wetting my bed and refusing to speak to visitors, even close relations. Although my mother and Nanny tried to make excuses for my behaviour, I knew only too well what they were thinking. Mrs This and Auntie That were no doubt glad to be rid of my company when finally, Nanny ordered me upstairs.

I soon realised I could never win by these tactics and came to the conclusion that since my brother was the sole cause of all the trouble, he and he alone should be made to pay for my unhappiness. Why go on venting my spleen on outsiders who were in no way involved and who only disliked me all the more for these methods of trying to attract their attention from him to me? So I decided to change the strategy. I would embark on an intensive course of teasing, which would spoil his temper and make him cry. Spurred on by this childish jealousy, I would wait until Nanny's attention was otherwise engaged and creep quietly up to the cot or pram, pinch or slap his hands, awaken him with a start by sudden loud noises or frighten him by making the most hideous faces I could think of. Cecil still continued to be the good sweet baby he had always been, but Nanny became very cross. If anything, the only temper I spoiled was hers.

One day, exasperated beyond measure, she seized my destructive hands, shut me in a dark cupboard on the landing and locked the door, hoping that this drastic punishment would aptly fit the crime and perhaps teach me a lesson for all time. Shutting children in cupboards was a common Victorian method of chastisement, but one Nanny had, up to that time, rightly shunned. I was truly terrified, beating my fists against the wall, screaming to her to let me out and kicking wildly against the spot where a gleam of light showed up the outline of the door. "I'll never be naughty again" I promised. At that moment, I was prepared to promise anything for freedom, and never to be naughty again was just about the ultimate offer I could make. For a little while (and it was only a little while, but it felt like years) no one came, and sobbing hysterically, I threw myself on the dusty floor and banged my head on the boards until a long splinter cut my forehead and the blood ran into my eyes. It was not many minutes before Nanny opened the door and released me, but the frightening experience taught me a salutary lesson. Cecil was not teased again.

I was not totally cured, however. Deciding it was useless to try to compete with Cecil for the affection and admiration I had considered to be my sole right, I tried a new stratagem: I would show the world how little I CARED. From then on, I would become as rude as I dared, short of inviting further punishment. My mother's friends' dislike of such an unattractive child showed on their expressions and in their comments, much to her mortification, but as far as I was concerned, if they did not like me, well TOO BAD! I could not care less. Secretly of course, I did care, dreadfully.

One person to see under the bravado and who had sufficient perception to understand that here was merely an unhappy little girl was dear Aunt Bessie, my father's kind eldest sister. When she went out of her way to be especially nice to me, I could not help but respond. The result was that I positively overwhelmed Aunt Bessie with affection and gratitude that must have bordered on embarrassing sometimes, and when she visited us, would not let her out of my sight for a moment.

Aunt Bessie endeared herself to me still more once by bringing me a bunch of white flowers for my birthday instead of a toy. This might not have occurred to some people as being a present, and it boosted my ego no end. I longed to do something for her in return, but could not think of anything she might want, until one evening, just before bedtime, an idea came to me.

Although very fond of children, Aunt Bessie did not have any. Her husband, Uncle Morris, was prim and proper, tidy and somewhat pompous, and he probably preferred it so. She must be very lonely I thought, rattling around in her large, cold house, which, now I come to think of it, must have been stuffed full of treasures. Morris Miles was a knowledgeable man in the art world and a collector of valuable paintings, many of which were donated to a local museum after his death. But what were a few dusty old oil paintings to the joy of a baby? From the experience of Cecil's arrival, I could see that a baby must be the supreme gift. I would have liked to have given her Cecil, but this would have proved difficult and stealing somebody else's baby had its disadvantages, since I might be found out.

Prayer was the only answer. That night, I earnestly exhorted the Almighty in my bedtime prayers to "please send Aunty Bessie a baby". "That should do it" I thought. Miracles did not enter my calculations, and not surprisingly, in this instance, God did not respond.

Aunt Bessie died very suddenly one day while visiting London and I grieved for her for many months afterwards.

And that Cecil was still around. When Nanny took us both out in our double pram, he with his halo hat on, he looked so angelic that strangers stopped to ask whose was the beautiful baby. I, totally ignored, of course simply stared with black looks. Beautiful? Huh!

Mother used to come and tuck me up every evening after I had been put to bed. I slept alone now and it was one of the few times I had her completely to myself. But here was the chance for another ploy. Whenever possible, I deliberately wet my bed just before her arrival. Then, after she had seated herself down on the counterpane and was about to kiss me a tender goodnight, I would lay my hand on her arm, tug at the lacy sleeve and with a fiendish expression, look into her eyes and say brightly: "I done it again". I would gloat wickedly at the shocked look on her usually serene countenance.

After the experience in the cupboard, I became afraid of the dark. When I was considered old enough to sleep by myself, I developed a new fear, of night-time furniture, common I am sure among children in that era. The room chosen for me was quite light and cheerful by day, but the many pieces of massive mahogany furniture made it look dark and forbidding and in the flickering shadows of the nightlight, even menacing. Lying in bed, I used to be fearful that during the night when I was asleep, a wardrobe or tallboy would move quietly over to my bed and crush me. In order to placate the furniture, having always been taught that politeness costs nothing, I would sit up in bed, bow solemnly to each piece in turn and say goodnight. I would then glance uneasily around to make sure that nothing looked like moving and eventually go off to sleep.

As Cecil grew older, I became reconciled to his presence in the household and we eventually became good friends. He was after all, only two years younger than me. When my father had his dinner parties, contrasting to my poor mother's incapacity, we were both full of beans and even when quite small, we would creep out of bed in our nightclothes, run to the landing and peer enviously through the balustrade at the constant stream of glamorous arrivals in the hall below.

One such glamorous visitor, frequently invited, was a Doctor Stanley Colyer, a cousin of my mother. He would bound up the stairs, come into my room, sit down on the bed and launch into a stream of questions as to what Cecil and I had been getting up to. He took such a kindly and avuncular interest in all our doings and escapades that I promptly fell in love with him, although I was only about six at the time. Being a very precocious child, when he promised to marry me when I grew up, I pleaded with him to be sure and wait for me. Then I would climb onto his lap, pull at his bow tie and hug and kiss him.

Ten years later, I still wanted to marry him, so he asked my parents if they thought the great age gap mattered all that much. He was then just about to take a post in South Africa. My parents answered most emphatically that indeed it did and much to my sorrow, he soon afterwards married a much older girl and they sailed away to a new life in a new continent. He died there at a comparatively early age some years later. I missed him terribly and looking back, I probably also missed the large wink he gave my parents when asking about the age gap, but I will always remember his good looks and wonderful voice. He was a lovely and very lovable man.*

*Dr Stanley Colyer was the brother of Sir Frank Colyer KBE FRCS FDSRCS Eng., the well-known dental surgeon, after whom the Colyer Institute got its name. Stanley was a radiologist and like his brother, published medical books and articles. The two brothers collaborated on various projects. The Royal College of Surgeons in London has a large collection of the Colyer brothers' material.

It was about a year after Cecil's birth that we moved house. Our first home, Number 26, was built at right angles to the road in the middle of a large flower-filled garden and was a lovely place, but only rented, from a retired doctor. Our second, Number 29, was an ugly four-storey building with iron railings guarding stone steps leading to a labyrinth of basements below. The house rose straight from the pavement to a height of some sixty feet, ending with an uneven roof and soot-encrusted chimneys. The basement housed the kitchen. Mother took one look at these and promptly ordered a bright airy new extension to be constructed on the ground floor. Good builders, vying with one another for their reasonable commissions, arrived on the dot and the work was faultlessly done and completed in record time. And no planning permission needed!

The new kitchens were built with a flat roof. When we were older – and should have known better – Cecil and I would climb onto it and, hiding in the shadow of the main wall, throw pebbles, orange peel and pieces of paper at passers-by and even spit on them, much to their understandable indignation and astonishment. I have to admit that I was almost certainly the instigator of these crimes.

The violent pealing of the front-door bell, followed by the sound of angry voices, meant that without a doubt, our hideout and identities had been discovered. Our victims had complained bitterly of the rude and undisciplined children at Number 29 and my mother was highly mortified. Needless to say, we received our due deserts.

The new kitchens did not improve the outside appearance of the house, but they made a great difference to the health and comfort of the staff. They could now sit in a bright warm room opening onto a secluded part of the garden at the back, and meals were prepared with far greater ease on the latest type of cooking stove. My mother, unlike some employers of the time, could never see why her staff should not enjoy as good conditions of living and comfort as herself, which was probably the reason some of them stayed with us for many years.

Although Cecil and I spent most of our days in the nursery with Nanny, on Sunday afternoons, washed and brushed up, Cecil in a clean suit and I in a white party frock, tied round the waist with a wide pink or pale blue silk sash, were taken down to the drawing room for afternoon tea with our parents and any visitors who might be staying, or who had dropped in. Often these were relations, for ours was a large family abounding with aunts, uncles and cousins, first, second and third, with goodness knows how many 'once removed' ones. We had to behave well in that room, for there was hardly space to move around, let alone run about.

Spindly chairs and small delicate tables crowded with valuable china ornaments were dotted around, and a grand piano covered with a velvet cloth trimmed with bobbles and long trailing curtains at the windows were pitfalls for little feet and exploring hands. Arranged carefully on the piano covering were even more ornaments, silver vases and framed photographs. I fear that cloth must have been pulled off, with dire results, more than once.

The front door of the house opened onto a passage leading via a right angle to the spacious square hallway. Drawing room, dining room, breakfast room, lobby and later, the new kitchen quarters, opened off it, in that order. At the far end, a wide staircase led to the bedrooms on the first floor. Pictures and portraits in oils hung everywhere.

Turkish and Persian carpets covered most of the floor space and nearly all the windows were draped with dense cream or coffee-coloured lace and heavy maroon or velvet curtains, allowing precious light to penetrate. Every downstairs room boasted 'Lincrusta' panelling halfway up the walls, dark flowery or formal patterned paper above and a massive fireplace bordered by an ornamental brass fender holding enormously long implements.

Despite numerous fires (both upstairs and downstairs), kept going in ineffectual register grates, the house in winter was usually freezing. Illumination everywhere was by gaslight, augmented here and there by a candle or two or a smelly oil lamp. Gaslight was all very well when the volatile incandescent mantle was new, as it then gave out a clear white light, but a touch in the wrong place or a sudden gust of wind always caused it either to burn dimly on one side only or be extinguished completely. The housemaid used to come up at about 6.30 on winter evenings to turn off the light after I had been finally tucked up for the night. Sometimes she would turn the tap the wrong way and send the bluish flame darting up to the ceiling and blackening the paint, and that was almost as alarming as being left in total darkness. I was allowed a night-light placed high out of reach in a saucer of water, but I did not relish the queer shadows it cast, particularly when a sudden gust of wind blew its tiny flame about.

The excitement of moving and of being established in a new home in a different nursery and with a larger garden to play in had done much to reconcile me to Cecil's existence, and as time went by, the brotherly thorn pricked less and less. Toys were shared and quarrels grew less frequent. Outings with Nanny and the preparations thereof were a major operation. For walks in summer, Cecil usually wore a white sailor suit, white socks and strapped shoes. I had to change into a clean starched white or pale blue frilly dress, light woollen coat, linen hat, blancoed shoes and lacy white socks. In winter, we were both muffled up to the eyebrows and fitted gaiters had to be buttoned over stockinged legs.

Party preparations were worse. So starched were my lacy frocks that fully dressed, I emerged as untouchable as an elaborately-iced wedding cake. I had to remain standing while Nanny tied bows of pink or blue ribbon on my ringlets (curls created in some discomfort during the previous night by rags tied in hard knots all over my head). Then came a wide sash with a long fringe which was my pride and joy, tied in a big bow at the back. When finally dressed and ready, I was not allowed to as much as fetch a doll from the toy cupboard or sit down on a nursery chair to look at a book (the chair might have been sticky). Nanny was a martinet where dress and decorum were concerned and was the most awful snob. We were never allowed to play with children she did not approve of, in case we caught some dreadful disease or, worse, learned BAD WORDS!

My father, like many another man, ducked out of the job of punishing us for our peccadilloes and would get out of it (when we appealed to his judgement and wisdom) by chiding us mildly and with mock severity informing us that our behaviour was "against the laws of the Medes and Persians". Who these strange people were we never knew and never asked, but as they did not appear too unfriendly, their strictures did not bother us unduly.

Apart from outings with Nanny, which did not count as they were merely extensions of nursery routine, our entrance into the outside world was via the dancing school run by the Misses Bird. There were three sisters in the Bird School of Dancing, all of them of the same stature, small, plump and with thin little legs, which made one wonder if they or their surname had come first. They were wonderfully energetic and were responsible for countless shows and school dancing displays in the town, besides teaching dancing - ballet and ballroom - in schools throughout the region. Miss Helen, the boss, ran her dancing class like a sergeant major. There were no concessions whatever to the tender age of her pupils (I was three when first enrolled) and she would rap out orders in stentorian tones, frightening the more nervous ones and eliciting loud clucks of disapproval from the nannies seated round the floor. But those among her students who were brave enough to stay the course soon realised that her bark was worse than her bite.

Miss Helen's sister, Miss Edith, dutifully echoed every order, but in far gentler tones. That she was afraid of the more forceful Miss Helen was all too apparent, and quite obviously she did not dare to disagree with her openly. The third member of the trio was Miss Kate, the pianist. She thumped out dance tunes almost non-stop on her long-suffering instrument, but in all the years I knew her, I never heard her utter a single word.

Miss Helen would point a thin leg, her foot encased in a black pump, ballet style with crossed straps and yell to her subdued row of pupils "chassé, chassé!" and a long line of little feet would attempt clumsily to do her bidding. Attendance at the Misses Bird dancing classes was indeed a traumatic experience.

The highlight of the year was the annual matinee held in the Grand Theatre around Christmas, and all three sisters, together with their conscripted labour force of sometimes unwilling pupils, worked untiringly for the success of that important afternoon. The theatre was always full. Local dignitaries, headed by the Mayor, would put in an appearance and hosts of proud mothers, fathers, aunts, uncles and cousins, plus their many friends and anyone else who could be coerced into coming, also attended. Every item on the programme was of course loudly applauded, but it was always the uncoordinated antics of the little ones, dressed as fluffy chickens, pussycats etc, that attracted the most enthusiasm.

The producers of the show knew their business and were totally dedicated, but their popularity rating was rather low among the nannies at their classes. Miss Helen had a way of trying to entice the small ones away from their protectors in order to join their bigger brothers and sisters on the floor by taking hold of their hands and pulling them towards her. Most would then burst into tears and try to cling to their nannies, burying their heads into highly-indignant bosoms or laps. But Miss Bird was not to be outdone. She usually succeeded in recruiting a sufficient number of bunnies, chickens and pussy cats for her annual show.

In due course, my brother Cecil joined the classes, welcomed warmly by the Misses Bird, for most boys hated dancing and were at a premium, especially for the famous matinees in which they would be called upon to take the parts of kings, knights or pages. Cecil was no exception to the general male dislike of dancing, but was given little choice in the matter.

CHAPTER THREE

FRIENDS AND RELATIONS

Our greatest friends (and that included the grown-ups) were the families of two local doctors. One family lived opposite to us in Carlton Crescent. They were the Aldridges, who had two girls, Phyllis and Joan, one younger and one older than myself and a boy, Raymond. Their house was very similar to ours, but they did have a very large and beautiful day nursery on the top floor with a huge bay window. The children owned a wonderful Noah's Ark with which we never grew tired of playing and occasionally quarrelling over. They had an extremely strict nanny who insisted that each animal should be carefully wrapped in cotton wool after the game was finished and everything returned to its proper place. Perhaps this is why there are so many beautifully preserved Victorian toys around today.

The other doctor's family, the Farquharsons, had only one daughter, Jean, and three sons, Stuart, Maurice and Ian, all of whom became doctors themselves. The Farquharsons owned a house in the Isle of Wight and we spent many a holiday there together enjoying uproarious games of cricket on the sands of an evening with our respective parents when the tide had gone out and the beach was flat and hard. Mornings and afternoons would be spent paddling, bathing and digging deep holes for the sea to run into. Such were the simple pleasures of a Victorian childhood. I thought the boys very handsome and great fun to be with. Jean I did not get on so well with, but she always tagged along. Poor Jean. I know now how she felt with no sister to redress the balance.

I have always loved cats, and I was given a little kitten called Penny. One day, thinking she would enjoy a ride in a lift, I put her in a small box, tied the end of a long ball of string round it, stood on the top landing of our house and pulled the box up the steep well of our stairs. Halfway up, she scrambled out and fell to the ground, miaowing piteously. My father came running at the noise and picked her gently up, furious with me for my stupidity. This was one time when the laws of the Medes and Persians were not invoked. Something stronger was called for on this occasion. Fortunately, Penny was not hurt, but it taught me a salutary lesson in consideration for animals.

Some Sundays were designated 'Grandma's Day', when we were taken by my mother on a visit to her parents, who lived in Fremantle, a Southampton suburb. Grandpa Ince was rarely in evidence on these occasions. I think he was a little afraid of children. 'Grandma with the Dogs', as we called her, was always waiting for us in her drawing room attended by a number of yapping Pomeranians. Entering her house was a feat of endurance and careful manoeuvring. We loved dogs, but not the canine volcanoes that met us at the door with their ferocious barking, dancing wildly at our feet and snapping at our white-socked ankles. When we at last made it to the front parlour, sidling in with our backs to the wall, our nerves were in a state of near exhaustion. Evidently, the dogs shared their master's dislike of children. Once in the presence of their mistress, the beastly animals leapt onto Grandma's lap, at least as many of them as could find room, and there was comparative calm.

Born in 1843 and the daughter of a London veterinary surgeon, Grandma could not have been all that old when we visited her as children, but to us she seemed so. She was an autocratic lady, dressed in old-style Victorian garb, making no concessions to fashion. "Sit here, boy!" she would say sternly to Cecil and "you, Kathleen, over there!"

indicating our respective seating arrangements. A tray of milk and soda and caraway seed cake would be brought in. "Now eat it all up and drink your milk slowly. Be careful not to make any crumbs. When you have finished you may go out and play in the garden." Grandma always gave the orders. Lesser fry and younger generations respectfully deferred.

Her outlook on current fashions extended to the décor of her house. It was furnished in the style of the 1880s, perhaps earlier, and remained untouched until she died at the age of ninety-eight. By then, it must have taken on the aura of a museum. But the gloom of the parlour gave way to a sunny conservatory onto which it opened. This boasted a large and prolific grapevine and with the pungent aroma of tomato plants and geraniums, it was a pleasant place (this was Grandpa's territory).

Released at last from the august presence of Grandma, we would run down the garden path leading to the Dell (as it was called) at the bottom. It was a long, narrow and steeply-sloping garden and growing anything in it must have been difficult, but the path was flanked by neat vegetable and flower beds almost down to the end, which was a shrubbery. There, right at the very end, was the fence bordering the railway line, high enough, fortunately, to discourage any thought of climbing it. Cecil and I always made a bee-line for this part of the garden, for there was the great thrill of watching the trains on their way to and from Southampton West Station.

At the first distant sound of an approaching locomotive, the game was to rush madly down once more to the bottom of the garden, hoping we would make it in time for the grand view.

Breathless with excitement, we waited for the distant rumble that heralded the approach of the express and then the staccato puffing which told us it was getting near. At last, like a burst of thunder, smothered in white smoke, the engine appeared, followed by its many carriages. The train rushed by and within minutes, all was quiet again. We might have been lucky enough to see two or more trains while the visit to Grandma lasted and while the grown-ups were gossiping.

Grandma's residence, Millbrook House, was from the outside as sedate as she was and had a dignified yucca plant in the middle of a carefully-tended lawn. The house was demolished some time ago to make way for the present-day industrial estate, or part of it.

When it was time to go home, Nanny would call us in from the garden, put on our coats and we would then make our polite farewells to Grandma standing at the front gate with my mother. It was a great relief not to have to return to the parlour and its formality. She and Grandfather had four daughters - Violet (my mother), Blanche, Dorothy (Dolly) and Maud. There was one son, Arthur.

Maud married a Norwegian lawyer called Carl Bagge and settled in Oslo. We seldom saw her and hardly knew our cousins, Astrid and George, for their visits to this country were very infrequent. During the Second World War, Maud, her daughter Astrid, who was then married, and her baby daughter had a terrible time after the Germans invaded. They were forced to hide in the mountains during a Norwegian winter with scarcely any food or warmth.

Blanche liked men and made no bones about it, which was considered a very bold attitude at the beginning of the 20th century. She also had a penchant for clergymen and married the Rev. Harry Cleife, whose living was at Hardington Mandeville in Somerset. They occupied an enormous old-fashioned vicarage containing countless old rooms which were impossible to fully furnish and they were also saddled with acres of garden, most of it a wilderness. We always enjoyed staying with them and got on very well with their two pretty daughters, Dorothy and Pen, and later a younger one, Vera. We were allowed more freedom there than at home and the four of us became friends with the sons of the gardener and groom, who joined wholeheartedly in our wild games, rushing all over the ample gardens. They took us to their respective homes, where we were able to view the latest litter of kittens or puppies or a newly-born calf in the nearby field. The country air did us 'townies' a power of good.

Unfortunately, Blanche was left a widow when still quite young. In his will, her husband had stipulated that if she was to inherit his estate, she must not remarry outside the Church. But a single existence did not suit Blanche. She needed a husband in her life. Consequently, she dragged her three daughters and their nanny all over the country to places where the incumbent of the parish might be an eligible bachelor. She became entangled with a bogus clergyman who tricked her out of some money, and not being a very good judge of character, she was easy prey. The attendant nanny had far more common sense and sent an urgent message to my father explaining the situation and relating her fears for the hapless Blanche. My father straightaway journeyed to wherever the family were at the time and managed to extricate his sister-in-law from a potentially unsuitable alliance. Blanche was finally married to a very sober, serious and highly respectable man, the Rev. Thomas Knight of St Albans, and settled down to the life of parish activities at Wickham Bishops, Essex, where she lived out her days in tranquil sobriety.

On my father's side of the family, there were quite a large number of children. He had three brothers, James, Thomas and Benjamin, and four sisters, Bessie, Annie, Margaret and Alice. My paternal grandparents both died before I was born. My father's mother (Eliza Goater before she married), with her companion Hatty, lived for a while in a separate suite of rooms at our first house, 26 Carlton Crescent. By all accounts Eliza was a dear old lady, liked by everyone, and although she was always glad of a visit from her son and daughter-in-law, she never interfered or gave unsolicited advice. Some years before her death, she became totally blind, which affliction, together with her increasingly painful arthritis, she bore without complaint.

Uncle James (junior) married twice, his offspring from the first marriage being a son, Harry, and a daughter, Hilda (referred to as 'poor Hilda' by the rest of the family). When their mother died, James made the great mistake of marrying a somewhat hard woman. Hilda was continually nagged and made into a complete drudge by her uncaring stepmother, but Harry came off even worse. He was timid and shrinking by nature, but Aunt Elsie forced him to join the Merchant Service, a hard taskmaster in those days and totally unsuited to his nature. Unable to withstand the pressures she put upon him, he signed on and was sent overseas and was never heard of again. It was generally believed he fell victim to a fever in some outlandish spot. His father and Hilda never forgave her for her pitiless treatment of him, but she cared little for people's opinions, even theirs.

Uncle James was a placid and kindly soul, but when she tried to keep the rest of his family out of their house in Rockstone Place, even he finally put his foot down and she angrily relented, but she kept out of the way whenever our voices were heard outside the front door. The house was very ugly and extremely inconvenient. Tall and narrow, it had a dark basement kitchen and just the one room on each floor. There were acres of oilcloth everywhere and the place was very cold in winter. At the front, it faced the featureless brick wall of the barracks opposite, but at the back, there was a pleasant open view of the Convent High School gardens.

Hilda grew up ministering to her parents' every need and had no life of her own at all. Then it was considered the right thing for a daughter to do and the fact that she might be merely an unpaid servant was usually unquestioned. In that house, 'poor Hilda' must have had her work cut out."★

★*The census records give a little more information about this family. In 1891, James was living at Strathearn, Westwood Road, South Stoneham with his first wife Agnes and children Henry G. aged six, and Hilda M., aged four. There were three servants - Emily Gee from Portesham, Dorset aged 23 who was the cook, Nancy Gee, nurse domestic aged 26 from Portesham and Agnes Ida Rood, aged 19, from Southampton, housemaid domestic. The 1901 census shows James, a widower, now living at his uncle's old address in Rockstone Place with just his son and daughter and a slightly reduced domestic staff, Frances Bower Story, aged 58, who was the cook and Ellen Lane, aged 16, housemaid.*

1911 tells a different story. There are James and Elsie, his new wife, aged 50 (he was 65), no Henry, Hilda and just one general servant, Anne Emily Hall from Fulham, Middlesex aged 78, so presumably, Hilda must have taken over the cooking and a good deal of the housework. It was a pity her father could not have stood up to his domineering wife a bit more and made things easier for his poor children. He had married Elsie Rolls in 1902.

Annie, Father's second sister, married a Joseph Summers, a civil engineer, at Kensington in 1879 and had two sons Francis Joseph (Frank) and Owen, and a daughter, Florence, known to everyone as 'Flossie'. Frank was married to a very delicate wife and spent most of his life at Newent in Gloucestershire. Flossie stayed there also and married fairly late in life a bank manager, moving with him to Ryde in the Isle of Wight. We saw a lot of both these cousins. My mother was very fond of Flossie, who had a breezy, jolly outlook on life and a great sense of humour. She often came to stay with her 'Aunt Vi', leaving husband Fred to the ministrations of two good maidservants, faithful retainers who had been with the family for most of his life. Fred and Flossie had a son and a daughter.

Just after the end of the 1939/45 war Flossie's son Michael, a serving officer in the RAF, was returning home to be demobbed when his plane crashed into a mountain in dense fog in the North African desert. He and his four companions, who had come through the war unscathed, were all killed instantly. Poor Flossie was completely heartbroken. She and Michael had always been very close and she had so looked forward to having him home again safe and well. He had always been the kindest and most considerate of sons and in spite of the deepest sympathy shown to her by everyone, for a time she felt her own life was at an end.

At the time of this tragedy, she was already a widow. Her daughter Yvonne was married and living in South Africa. At the latter's pressing invitation, she straightaway packed everything and left England for Port Elizabeth where Yvonne lived, to try and make a new life for herself. But it was a long time, if ever, before she was able to get over the shock of Michael's death.

Chapter Four

International tensions

After about six years with us, Nanny left to live with an older sister and thus continue her selfless life of service to others, as her sister was ailing and unable look after herself. We missed her immeasurably. A hundred times a day we wanted to run and ask her something, to find lost toys, to explain things, and she was no longer there. My mother did her best, but we still felt completely lost without the person who had been so much the rock of security in our young lives. Cecil and I went to stay with her for brief periods when she had settled down in her new home, but her sister did not take kindly to two strange children cluttering up her immaculate cottage, so in spite of once more being in the company of our beloved guardian angel, we never stayed long.

The time had now come when our education had to be thought about, and not long after Nanny's departure, a French friend of my mother's, Mademoiselle Marie Bernigaud from Paris, arrived to help out and teach us her language. Hot on her heels came a German girl, Kate Ebert, who joined the household as German tutor. Allied to them was a prim little governess engaged to teach us the rudiments of reading, writing and simple arithmetic.

Mademoiselle never endeared herself to me. She was altogether too strict and unbending, but she introduced me to the works of Madame de Savigny - *La Bibliothèque Rose, Les Malheurs de Sophie, Les Petites Filles Modèles, Les Memoirs d'un Ane* and lots more, and I am grateful to her for this. Many happy hours I spent, aided by Kate, cutting out a doll's trousseau taken from designs in one of those French books.

The twin demons of jealousy and insecurity must have resurfaced in me after Nanny left us and perhaps it was the gap in our lives caused by her absence, but from the time I learned the German for "do you love me?" poor Kate was plagued by an eager voice following her around several times a day asking "liebst du mich?" She must have been heartily sick of constantly having to answer "Ja, ja".

Mademoiselle, although strictly unbiased in any discrimination between Cecil and myself, showed little affection towards anyone. She was religious to the point of fanaticism and considered human emotion of any sort undesirable, so I soon decided time spent trying to ingratiate myself would be entirely wasted. She was a Catholic and considered the world totally evil, and few things, in her estimation, escaped the label of sinfulness.

At first language lessons were given to me alone as Cecil was still quite young, but while playing on the nursery floor, he managed to pick up nearly as much French and German as I learned from personal instruction and from text books. It stood him in good stead during the Second World War, for while serving in the RAF and able to speak fluent German. One of his duties as Adjutant on the Isle of Sheppey was to interrogate in their own language enemy pilots shot down during the Battle of Britain.

The four of us and my parents (the governess did not accompany us) spent Easter and summer holidays on the Isle of Wight. My father owned three houses in Sandown. This was not quite as affluent as it sounds, since houses then were cheap and easy to buy. They were called Oxford Cottage, Glenarm and Royal Heath Cottage. I wonder if they still exist? Anyway, we had ready-made accommodation for our stays on the Island. In the early 1900s Sandown was a different place from its modern counterpart. The sands were clean and white, the sea unpolluted and sparkling. There were few hotels, no camp or caravan sites, no fish and chip parlours and nothing to mar the beauty of a completely unspoiled seaside resort.

We used to embark from Southampton on one of the old paddle steamers - it might have been the *Queen,* the *Solent Queen* or the *Balmoral* - and they left from the Town Quay. We docked at Ryde, took a little train to the end of the pier and then boarded another train, journeying through lovely countryside to Sandown.

We were very spoilt. One or two of the servants would always go over to prepare the chosen house in advance of our arrival to air the beds and to take over the heavy luggage and necessary kitchen utensils. This made the journey practically trouble-free and as enjoyable as the holiday itself. We were met at Sandown Station by an ancient cabby who drove us to the cottage, and we children were hardly within the door before we were pestering the grown-ups to take us down to the beach. Our doctor's family, the Farquharsons, who often took their holidays at the same time, would rush over to join us on hearing the noise of our arrival, and we would all organise a game of cricket on the wide expanse of sand. They were wonderful days and the weather was always hot and sunny, or so it seemed.

At Easter, we would spend more time exploring the countryside and sometimes picnicking. Away from the coast, the whole place would be a riot of colour, the woods and fields a solid carpet of primroses, violets and bluebells with kingcups flourishing in every damp spot and anemones fighting for space wherever they found an untenanted piece of mossy ground. At a place called Borthwood with the pale spring sunshine filtering through the tall trees, it was an enchanting sight. We would come home from picnics laden with bunches of drooping flowers, tired but happy.

Those halcyon days were not without their tragic side. Jake was our great friend. He belonged to one of the rival fishing factions and operated from his appointed territory, left of the pier. He was young, dark and handsome. He never minded hordes of children following him around asking endless questions while he gutted the fish and filled the wooden crates. Sometimes he even found time to tell us stories of his adventures, no doubt coloured a little in his imagination to make them sound even more exciting. Summer after summer he was always there, and we all thought the world of him.

Then one winter's evening, I overheard my father telling my mother that Jake had been drowned while fishing during a severe storm. For a full moment I stood at the door trying to take in the awful truth that our Jake was dead and we would never see him again, never see that good-looking face and never again hear his accounts of the amazing things that happened to a sailor on the high seas. I cried a lot at that sad news. Sandown had lost one of its chief attractions.

By way of a change, one year our parents decided we

would go to the Continent for the annual holiday. Kate and Marie were sent home to visit their respective families and my parents intended to holiday by themselves at Interlaken while we were despatched in the care of a new fräulein to stay at the home of friends living at Wiesbaden, who had children the same age as ourselves.

We travelled to our destination via Heidelberg, that beautiful medieval city on the banks of the Neckar. We had taken a little train which journeyed beside the river and passed through magnificent country rising on each side of the water. We gazed upwards in wonder at the fairy-tale castles appearing unexpectedly above the encircling pines on the steep hillside. It was like a pantomime backdrop. Were there giants, witches or princesses living up there?

Wiesbaden was very different from Heidelberg; a much more modern town. The surroundings however were lovely with woods, fields and pine forests abounding and steep green hillsides forming a perfect framework for the town itself. One young fräulein from the family we stayed with took us for long mushroom hunts in the local woods. She brought with her a coloured leaflet showing which fungi were edible and which poisonous. Nevertheless, some passers-by would express horror at seeing some of the harvest we had gathered and Fräulein was warned against letting us even touch some of them. Despite these dire warnings we never came to any harm.

The house itself was a rambling building set in the middle of a large and wild garden. With our host's children we played endless games of cops and robbers. Of course, it was always good-natured Cecil who was the one tied to a tree and fired at. He took it all in good part, as he did everything, and willingly consented to be the statutory victim and permanent stooge. At the end of three weeks, our parents returned from their Swiss holiday, collected us and we set off for home.

Holidays over, lessons in the schoolroom began again. Prim little Miss Preedy and the friend to whom she had handed over had both left and there followed in quick succession a series of rather colourless middle-aged ladies, none of whom made much impression either educationally or otherwise upon Cecil and me. Progress in speaking French and German did continue satisfactorily, helped on by the insistence of my mother, who was fluent in both languages, that one or the other should always be spoken at mealtimes in the dining room. Fine for her, and sometimes us, but not for my poor father, who did not understand a word of either and must have found his mealtimes consequently rather dull. She, Kate and Marie would chatter away to each other, leaving him and quite often, Cecil and me out in the cold.

About a year later, Kate returned to Germany to care for her old parents and her younger sister Lotte came to take her place. Lotte was as different a character from her gentle, kind and loving sister as chalk from cheese, and before she had been in the house a day, she took an instant and violent dislike to Marie Bernigaud. The latter reciprocated by avoiding her whenever possible and speaking to her only when absolutely necessary. Throughout the whole of Lotte's stay with us, the two remained at daggers drawn and the atmosphere in the nursery was as a result, extremely hostile.

Because Marie was rather staid and trim, Lotte played a trick on her which must have taken some careful planning and proved how much they disliked each other. I suspect that Lotte did not realise just how much hurt and disgust her prank would cause the sensitive and strait-laced Marie, but whether she did or not, her actions were hardly good examples to show to our young and impressionable minds. I must admit though that we thought it very funny when we heard about it later.

Cecil had a small chamber pot under his bed and this Lotte removed. She carefully wrapped it in brown paper and tied it with string, but took pains that its shape would be apparent to everyone. On the outside of the parcel she printed in large black letters "TEACUP. MADE IN FRANCE."

It was Marie's afternoon off when she usually took a tram down town to do some shopping. Lotte discreetly followed her with the parcel and trailing her as close as she dared, made sure she was not spotted. When the tram stop was reached, Marie entered the vehicle and was about to take her seat when Lotte, having run the last few yards, breathlessly reached the conductor as he was about to ring the bell. She handed him the parcel and in loud ringing tones that could be heard halfway up the Avenue, said: "Please give this to the lady sitting over there, she has left it behind and will soon be needing it urgently."

Another person with more sense of humour would have ignored so childish an escapade, but not poor Mademoiselle, who nearly fainted with humiliation and chagrin, while Lotte, completely unrepentant, ran back home laughing her head off. There were prolonged and tearful complaints made later to my mother when Lotte had recovered sufficiently to return home with the 'teacup', and it required all the tactful persuasion of both my parents to induce her to remain in the same house as Lotte. These of course were the days when Queen Victoria was still on the throne and such embarrassments, which nowadays would be laughed off as mere foolishness or just plain silliness, loomed large.

Lotte was severely reprimanded by my father and threatened with ignominious and instant repatriation minus references if she ever dreamed of playing any further jokes on anyone. This completely sobered her up, but

Marie refused to forgive her. I doubt if they ever spoke to one another again.

This incident, harmless as it was, affected Mademoiselle deeply and she continued to look very downcast and miserable. I went up to her one evening, put my hand in hers and offered her a small bunch of wild flowers I had picked on the Common that day. Neither of us said a word, but when she turned and smiled at me in thanks, there were tears in her eyes.

It was just as well then that Lotte was not to remain long with us in any case. Before she left Germany, she had become engaged to a young lieutenant - Hans. She was madly in love with him and this was probably one of the reasons she found it so difficult to settle in England. She was always homesick and then to cap it all, Hans suddenly stopped writing. Nothing would persuade her that there was not some other woman involved and when my mother, meaning well, told her not to worry and said "there are always other fish in the sea", Lotte burst into tears, rushed to her room and started packing. It was probably not the most tactful thing to have said to a lovesick girl and Lotte, determined she was not going to lose Hans, returned to Germany forthwith.

Marie and my mother had always got on well and she remained with us for several more years. With both Kate and Lotte gone, she continued to instruct us in French.

When she did eventually return to Paris, my mother visited her there from time to time and sometimes brought her back to stay with us. Marie did not live to make old bones however. An ambassador's carriage knocked her down one day when she was crossing a busy street in her home city. Always a fervent Catholic, she promised in her prayers to devote her remaining years to the Church if her life was spared. To a certain extent, she recovered from her injuries, but she was left a cripple. The convent to which she offered herself would not accept an invalid and she died soon afterwards as a sort of lay sister, working in a very menial capacity.

There were other eruptions in the household from time to time. We had a cook who when ordering gorgonzola cheese called it "golden solo" (a prettier name really). She was somewhat plain in appearance with a bun of straight lanky hair and she wore voluminous skirts. When Cecil was very small, he followed her upstairs one day and peeped under her petticoat (or one of them). She was furious and accused him to my mother of having evil designs on her, which was highly unlikely considering his age and her lack of beauty. But poor Cecil, not having the faintest idea what all the fuss was about, was punished for his rudeness.

When Marie was still with us, one morning after what had seemed a night of disturbance with much coming and going, she interrupted our nursery breakfast to tell us we had a baby brother. Although she looked weary, having probably been up all night, she smiled all over her normally severe face as she gave us the news. This time I was delighted at the prospect of having a new playmate and someone else besides Cecil to boss around, but the most pleased I think, was Cecil himself. At last, another boy! Someone to back him up against his frequently obstreperous sister. We were detailed off to impart the glad news to our nearest (geographically speaking) relatives, my uncle and aunt in Rockstone Place. On the way, passers-by were mildly surprised to see two children skipping along excitedly singing loudly *"Nous avons un petit frère, nous avons un petit frère!"*

Marie had accompanied us to our uncle and aunt's house (the aforementioned James and Elsie) and she rang the bell while we waited expectantly. When Aunt Elsie opened the door (and it was a pity it was her and not Uncle James) Cecil and I burst out with the good news. Totally ignoring us, my aunt turned to Marie and coldly enquired after my mother's health and on being reassured on that score, informed us frostily that she could not ask us in, as her sister Jessie (who lived with them) was not at all well and needed complete quiet. We turned, by this time somewhat subdued, and followed Marie down the steps. The door was immediately shut behind our backs. Even

Marie was *blessée* by the lukewarm reception of such glad tidings and the strange ways of some English people!

By the time of the birth of our new brother, we had moved house again, this time to a modern residence in Westbourne Crescent, situated off the Avenue, the wonderful broad highway that sweeps down from Bassett, then a country village, to the middle of the town. Pre-1914 and even pre-1939, Southampton was a pleasant and beautiful place to live in and was not the large conurbation we know today. Its main industry was shipping and beyond the scattering of handsome houses and small family businesses which made up the town centre, it was virtually rural. As in any large town, there were pockets of poverty and some districts were decidedly run-down, and although everyone knows you cannot live on fresh air alone, unlike other towns it was possible to escape from the misery of being poor, if only by going down to the foreshore and breathing the fresh tangy air of the Solent.

As children and with no need to escape from such an existence, we would clamber over the cannons on the Esplanade, peep through the wooden boards on the jetty to watch the green water sloshing against the supports and give Nanny heart attacks climbing the crumbling town walls as far as we dared. But once in Westbourne Crescent, the Common became our main playground.

When I reached the grand old age of eleven I was finally sent to school. It was a small private one situated in Archers Road and was run by a Mrs Lucas. The standard was not very high and I was able to keep up with the other pupils in most subjects. Thanks to Marie and Kate, I had no problems with French and German and was well ahead.

German was taught at the school by a Frieda L., a large, fiercely aggressive woman who must surely have been the fore-runner of the wardresses in Buchenwald or Belsen. Fräulein L. had some friends in Germany who were prepared to take a child as paying guest to improve its grasp of the language and learn something of their way of life. She persuaded Mrs Lucas to send her daughter Marian over there. This was agreed and Marian accordingly travelled to Germany and was there for the best part of a year. She was one of my favourites at the school. She was short, dark and sturdy with vibrant black curly hair and bright eyes the colour of ripe horse chestnuts. Her complexion was more Italian than English and I wondered if her father, long since dead, had come from Italy or Spain.

When Marian returned in 1912, we all clustered round asking questions non-stop about her life abroad, the people she had met and the things she had done. However, she seemed to be in a strangely reticent frame of mind and we did not learn a great deal from her. Although I could not elicit a great deal from her about her experiences in

Germany, because I hated to be outdone in anything I wanted to go there too. I pleaded with my parents to be allowed to sample a taste of going abroad on my own, just like Marian, the family she had stayed with apparently being willing to take another English girl. My parents had some misgivings, even though my mother had herself been to finishing school on the Continent. Eventually they agreed and so, accompanied by an elderly but trusted lady chaperone, I was seen off on the boat train at Harwich.

On the boat, we had a tiny cabin occupied by two other ladies and I found it difficult to sleep owing to the stuffiness in the small space and to insect bites which caused constant scratching and scalp irritation. I hesitate to speculate just what these insects were, but they were certainly hungry! We arrived early next morning at Bremerhaven, tired and dishevelled with little appetite for the breakfast set before us, but glad that the major part of the journey was over.

Chapter Five
Anglo-German hostilities

Once we had disembarked and had our luggage, a fairly long train journey brought us to Bückeburg Station, where Herr E. awaited us. He had been waiting a long time and the weather was cold, so maybe his gloomy unsmiling face was not so surprising. What did slightly worry me was the fact that his expression did not change even when, after saying goodbye, thank you very much and bon voyage to my kindly companion, he drove me to his house without saying a single word. I felt shy and could think of nothing to say, and found his tight-lipped and stern presence inhibiting.

Thus, in complete silence, we were driven swiftly to a tall grey building on the main street. He motioned me to get out, then proceeded to mount some stone steps leading to a dingy front door which he unlocked and opened wide before returning to get my luggage. The hall we entered exuded that dank smell redolent of dry rot or rising damp. It was dark but looked clean and the oilcloth was well polished. From the shadows, a tall thin woman dressed in black emerged and came towards me unsmiling. *"Guten Morgen Fräulein, willst du bitte nach oben kommen, und ich werde dich dein Zimmer zeigen"* (I'll show you your room). She motioned me to bring up my two heavy suitcases. Herr E. meanwhile vanished into the back regions as soon as his wife appeared.

I was led to a door on the first floor. We entered together and I dumped my cases on the bed, then turned to her. To my astonishment, instead of the long-delayed welcome, she went out again, shut the door firmly and left me alone to unpack without uttering another word.

The room was cold and bare, the only window placed high up and tightly shut. There was a camp bed, a chest of drawers, a rickety chair and a corner wardrobe consisting of a plain curtain covering a triangle of space. On the floor were two worn rugs, one on each side of the bed. A wave of homesickness flooded over me, bringing hot tears to my eyes. I wished with all my heart that the clock could be put back a month, a week, even 24 hours, and I could be back home with my loving family in our bright and happy home. What made the whole thing worse was that I had asked, begged to come here. What a terrible mistake! I realised now why Marian had been so reluctant to talk about her experiences. Here was I, also marooned in this unfriendly household with no one near whom I knew and in a strange country.

War between England and Germany was looming on the horizon and even at the age of thirteen, I sensed the sinister undercurrents that were beginning to permeate the country in which I was a guest. At the time, a fanatical love of the Kaiser burnt in the breasts of most of his countrymen. He was indeed an imposing and martial figure. I saw him once when he visited Bückeburg en route for some more important town. The whole population turned out to welcome him and everyone went down on their knees reverently when he rode through the main street on horseback in his green Jaeger uniform. Even I was impressed.

With the exception of the timid shadowy presence of the mother I had met when I first arrived, all the Es, from the hectoring bullying head of the house to the youngest daughter (seven-year-old Puppi), treated me very badly. Perhaps it was no coincidence that Frieda L. had been their friend.

The older sons of the household sometimes tried to maul me about and kiss me, but being lithe and quick, I usually managed to avoid being in their presence for more than a minute and would dart away as soon as I saw them coming or heard their voices in the distance.

Herta, the eldest girl, defied description. She had a peculiar penchant for hair-ribbons and in addition to annexing all I had brought with me, forced me to ask for more in nearly every letter I wrote home by means of pinching, scratching or hitting me hard where it hurt most or devising some other form of hateful punishment should I dare to disobey her orders. Being much younger and weaker than she was, I dared not go against her in any way. Needless to say, my mother was mystified by the frequent and unusual requests, but as my letters were carefully censored, I could mention nothing of my treatment.

Herta knew that war was not too far off, both from overhearing her parents' discussions and reading the screaming headlines on newsagents' boards. So one day, she decided to stage a rehearsal of war between our two countries and roped in her younger brother to assist. After briefing him no doubt to her full satisfaction, she chose a day when her parents were out and there was no one at home to hear the noise or to intervene. She then gave the signal for battle to commence. Bodo, who was about my own age, advanced menacingly towards me saying in a loud swaggering voice, "We are all coming over to England to shoot you, your mother and everyone else in your house all in a heap."

This was the sign for Herta to scream excitedly, giving me a hefty push towards her brother. "Go on, hit him!" she yelled and to Bodo "Go on, pull her hair out, slap her face!" When she was satisfied that we had both had a good bash at each other while she constantly yelled encouragement and we were exhausted and weeping, she would laugh like a maniac and leave the room.

Looking back, I suspect now that the word 'maniac' was not far from the truth. It seems to me that all could not have been right with her mental state, for she was so constantly bent on persecution. She was seventeen, going on eighteen, and for those days, very sexually advanced for her age. She obtained a sinister vicarious pleasure in observing other people's reactions to any particular form of torture she could devise. An instance of this was when she invited some young student friends to accompany us in walks through the dense pine woods near her home. When we had reached the thickest part of the forest, she struck. This time she had planned that I should be raped by one of her male companions. "Make love to her, go on go on!" she said, and tried to shove one or other of them towards me. "She won't know what it is all about, go on" was the persuasive cry.

I did not know what it was all about. All I knew was that Herta wanted something very nasty to happen. Fortunately, the boys concerned were too astounded to comply with her wishes, and before they could change their minds, I took to my heels and ran as fast as I could back to the house, screaming in fear and horror. I was trembling with shock by the time I reached it. I knew then, if I had not before, that I was living under the same roof as a she-devil.

I attended school with the Es' children. Our day started at 7.30 am in the summer and 8 am in winter, with most afternoons free or given over to games. I was by now fairly proficient in German and did not find learning lessons in a foreign language too difficult. We were taught all the usual subjects, including singing. The music teacher was a fiery woman who made a daily point of ordering the class to sing *Deutschland Über Alles* as loudly as possible. My patriotic rendering of 'England ber Alles' was noticed and I was told to report to her office. I do not remember the punishment, if any, that I received. It was probably merely a reprimand.

Ema Bowger, a girl at the school at the school who was much older than I was, noticed my loneliness and during recreation times, she put herself out to befriend me, but soon Herta got wind of this and forbade me ever to speak to Ema again under pain of some unspecified torture. Maybe it sounds cowardly, but I was so terrified of Herta by this time that I accordingly carried out her instructions and refused to take any notice of my kind friend after that, and did not dare to explain why. Ema was understandably hurt by my sudden change of attitude and I cried myself to sleep thinking how ungrateful she must think me. But now I felt things had got to a stage where something would have to be done and I would have to try to get away from Germany and back home. I could stand the Es no longer and was beginning to lose both appetite and sleep.

In bed at night I began to spend the dreary sleepless hours working out ways of escaping from Bückeburg. But what could a thirteen-year-old girl with no money do to achieve this aim? In addition to seeing that the frequent requests for hair ribbon were never forgotten, Herta censored all my letters very thoroughly. When she had to go out, knowing that I would undoubtedly take advantage of her absence to write in secret, she would detail Puppi to watch me. When she was given this assignment, the little girl's eyes would light up with malice and like a shadow, she would follow me everywhere until her sister returned.

Day after day I planned my escape from this 'concentration camp' until at last I hit upon a way of giving them both the slip. I wrote the usual letter dictated by Herta on this occasion, asking, among other things, if my parents would let me stay on in Germany because I was "so happy". Herta stood over me with that menacing look designed to instil fear and obedience to her wishes – or else. As usual, I did what I was told, but this was one of the times when she went out, leaving Puppi as gaoler.

Now, it seemed, was my chance. When she had gone, as instructed and with Puppi keeping watch, I addressed the envelope and it was duly sealed. Then, quick as lightning, before the child had time to realise what was happening, I seized my pen and a second envelope and dashed into the lavatory as if taken short with sudden diarrhoea. I pretended to have the most awful stomach ache and although Puppi rushed after me, having been told not to let me out of her sight, I was too quick for her.

I flung myself into the room and locked the door. Then I quickly slit open the unstamped envelope, took out the letter and wrote a desperate postscript at the bottom. "I don't want to stay on here I hate this place and am very miserable, Herta made me write all this." I put the letter back in the second envelope, addressed and sealed it and then pulled the lavatory chain to lend credence to my sudden seizure.

I emerged as nonchalantly as I could. Puppi, who was waiting outside, grabbed the letter, licked the stamp she had ready between her fingers, stuck it on firmly and immediately ran out to the post. I, meanwhile, breathed a deep sigh of relief while marvelling at the subterfuge needed to get away from this extraordinary family.

War was now becoming imminent and rumours could no longer be discounted, but the possibility of hostilities actually breaking out still seemed inconceivable to peace-loving people like my parents in far-off England. The first part of my letter therefore inclined them to consider allowing me to stay on with the Es a few months longer. But once they read the postscript written in large capitals, they immediately decided to make all arrangements for my return forthwith. Fortunately, they had a friend who was coming over from Germany to get married. This lady had already booked her passage from Bremen on the *Kronprinzessen Cecilia* of the Nord-Deutscher Lloyd line, and she managed to obtain a ticket for me on the same ship. This voyage turned out to be the last for this particular vessel. She was torpedoed and sunk at the very outset of war.

That last night with the Es was one of the happiest days of my life. I believe they were not altogether sorry to be saying goodbye to me. With war so near, they probably thought an English child staying with them might have been an embarrassment. I sensed that the psychopathic Herta was deeply disappointed at losing so easy and captive a prey to her sadistic machinations.

Frau E. came with me to the station. In my relief and excitement at leaving, I do not remember saying goodbye to any of them, nor they to me, and as soon as the train drew along the platform, I jumped aboard and settled myself as far from Frau E. as possible. She had been largely innocent in my treatment by the rest of the family, but so glad was I to be at last seeing the back of them that when the train began to move out I scarcely gave her a backward glance.

In the large Bremen waiting room, with a white rose pinned to the lapel of my coat as a distinguishing mark, I waited to meet my travelling companion. The German lady in question, young and pretty and also wearing a white rose, was not long in picking me out. As she was about to be married I guessed she was as excited and anxious to be off as I was.

She came up smiling, holding out her hand in greeting, but I was still in some sort of delayed shock from my experiences and committed the most awful gaffe. "I shall be glad to put my foot on German ground for the last time!" I burst out.

My escort was naturally taken aback. "Really?" was her astonished reply. "Well, perhaps I shall be glad to put mine back."

She had been, not surprisingly, offended by my unguarded remark and realising how rude I must have sounded, I did my best to make amends to her on the journey back to England.

I had plenty of time to reflect on the past few months. Because war had not been so near, Marian had probably fared better with the Es than I did. The house had been spotless, the meals beautifully cooked and served by Frau E. She worked without a break from morning to night for her ungrateful family, bullied by her overbearing husband and browbeaten by her two grown-up sons, Hans and Rudi, who openly despised her.

Most unfortunately, I started off on the wrong foot by arriving with, of all things, nits in my hair! What a humiliating start to a visit. I certainly had not picked them up before leaving home. Possibly the dusty headrests on the German train were to blame, but that did not mollify Frau E. Not a bit of it. To say she was horrified at discovering my disgraceful condition was putting it mildly. Without ado, I was scrubbed from top to toe. My hair was then scraped with a fine tooth comb until my scalp was scratched and sore and even bled. I was then made to wear a close-fitting turban of white linen soaked in vinegar, day and night.

They had liked Marian, I gathered. Whether she had reciprocated was another matter. But in any case, the hatred Germany later showed against the English was by no means as evident in 1912. For another thing Marian was free from lice. I lost out on both counts.

The first day I was considered fit to be allowed out with the other young Es was not a happy one, for by then, homesickness, enhanced by the disapproval I had apparently incurred because of my unfortunate infestation, weighed heavily upon me. The children took me to a local pâtisserie, where they relieved me of all my initial stock of marks and pfennigs to purchase chocolate and cream cakes with extra portions of cream. I was so unhappy and felt so low in spirits that I could swallow not a single bite of my portion.

But now that was all behind me and I was on my way home with Fräulein Grete. The crossing was very rough. Poor Grete hung on to her charge as long as possible, her face assuming an ever greener hue. At last she had to give in and retired to her cabin, too ill to bother about anything. As for me, so elated was I at the thought of going home, mal-de-mer bypassed me completely and instead of going to bed at the usual hour, I spent most of the night in the lounge, laughing, singing and dancing with the rest of the noisy, laughing crowd of passengers.

The first light of dawn broke on a storm-lashed sea. I had not bothered to undress and was lying tired but excited on the lower bunk. As we were due to dock in half an hour, I reminded my poor prostrate friend that she had better get a move on. She slid gingerly from her bunk to the floor and made her unsteady way to the bathroom for a perfunctory wash and brush-up before meeting her fiancé. The rolling and pitching of the ship gradually diminished and as the speed lessened, there was a shouting and running and clanking of chains overhead. The throbbing of the engines stopped altogether, and there came what seemed like a dead silence. I looked out of the porthole to see a great, grey stone wall. We were back in Southampton.

Poor dear responsible Grete, having somehow managed to pull our luggage together as well as herself, took my hand and guided me along the narrow passage and up the stairs to the gangway. A sea of faces gazed up at us from the dockside. A figure broke away from the crowd and began to wave violently in our direction. Grete's tired eyes lit up as she recognised her fiancé. Then I saw my mother, my father and my two brothers. It was one of the best moments of my life when I flung myself into their arms.

CHAPTER SIX

CONVENT LIFE

The events of the past year gradually faded into the mists of memory as new experiences began to unfold. I was now to be a fully-fledged schoolgirl in England and was enrolled at the Convent High School as a weekly boarder. I was again assailed by homesickness, despite being able to see my parents at weekends. I also found the convent food very stodgy and altogether did not care for my first term at all. There seemed to be interminable hours spent in the chapel and I was always forgetting to genuflect in front of the altar.

Because it was originally a French order of nuns, the sisters were addressed as 'Madam' (without the end 'e'). The Southampton convent (which was almost next door to our old house) had been founded about thirty years earlier and was of the order known as La Saint Union des Sacres Coeurs (usually referred to as 'LSU'). The nuns wore immaculate long black habits with white pleated wimples and wide white collars. A broad black ribbon round their shoulders supported a large metal cross, and rosaries hung from their waists. Peeping out beneath the full swishing skirts it seemed strange to see were what looked like men's black lace-up shoes, but fashion and vanity are not part of a nun's outfit.

Madam Imelda, who taught the upper forms, was a great character. Small and plain in appearance, she had very intelligent eyes and a lively expression. She was a natural teacher, but her thoughts would sometimes wander during a lesson and she would leave sentences unfinished in mid-air with the last word or two unspoken.

She had odd ideas as to how a lady should comport herself in her own home. It was apparently 'infra dig' to brush one's hair in the bedroom. "A lady should always go into the bathroom to do this and lock the door," she would say. She once took some of us shopping to Edwin Jones, a large draper's store at the bottom of the town. Seeing in the window a quite modest evening dress, she murmured: "But surely, dear, a blouse would always be worn underneath that frock."

I developed quite a crush on a French nun who taught music, Madam Hermanie. I remained devoted to her, no matter how cross she became during piano lessons when, so nervous in spite of hours of practice, my fingers felt like all thumbs. Quite a number of her pupils idolised her, so she must have had quite a deal of magnetism in her personality. Another nun I remember with affection was Madam Hortense, the German mistress. She was also a good teacher and popular too, not least because she was also in charge of the tuck shop.

Cecil was sent to Eastbourne College to complete his education. While there, he decided to follow in Father's footsteps and become a solicitor, the fourth generation in the family to do so. One of his daughters eventually also became one. He had two other children, both of whom became doctors.

When war came in 1914, as we were too young to take part, it affected us very little. I can remember no Zeppelin raids on Southampton and at the convent, we slept peacefully in our beds during the whole of the four years. But the linguistic ability of my silly Aunt Blanche nearly landed her into more hot water. She, my mother and the other sister had spent part of their school days on the Continent, as it was thought the right thing in those days for young ladies whose parents could afford it to be able to learn at least one or two languages other than their native tongue. When a trainload of German prisoners of war arrived at Southampton Station, Blanche, never averse to a male presence, excitedly rushed up to the train and shook hands enthusiastically one after another with the prisoners, meanwhile conversing volubly in German with them. She had either ignored or not seen a poster in the station forbidding such fraternisation, and she was arrested. It took all my father's powers of persuasion to convince the authorities that his impulsive sister-in-law was not a spy but merely a bit thoughtless. Blanche herself stated indignantly that if, as should have been the case, the people in charge had understood the language, they would have known she was only asking the soldiers what part of Germany they were from and how their families were coping at home.

Convent life impressed me more and more as time went by, and I became greatly attached to the nuns, their faith, their dedication and their way of life. So when I announced to my parents that I wanted to become a Catholic and eventually join the order, the news was not received with unalloyed enthusiasm. I had been sent to the convent because it had a well-deserved reputation, well beyond the confines of Southampton, for good teaching and getting its pupils through exams. It was a good deal cheaper too than my former school. These considerations weighed heavily on quite a few parents, Catholic or not, and consequently, the convent attracted many non-Catholic pupils, of whom I was one.

So my announcement of becoming a Catholic and taking the veil did not go down at all well. My father particularly disapproved. He had been at one time churchwarden at St Mary's, one of Southampton's oldest and most important C of E churches. The nuns themselves had done nothing to consciously encourage my aspirations. Madam Imelda, the Headmistress, was far too down-to-earth in any case to take any notice of teenage girls and their wild enthusiasms. Moreover, with the large number of non-Catholics at the school, she had to be extremely circumspect with regard to religious bias in order to avoid any accusations of pressure or brainwashing. This would have done the Convent's high reputation no good at all.

My parents, while grateful for the care and good education I was receiving, did not share my enthusiasms, so they decided that my growing tendencies for convent life must be curbed somewhat and that a change of school was called for. I was sent off to Winchester Girls' School for a year. This plan to take me away from my beloved convent was hard to take, but children did not then question parents' decisions and I therefore had to obey. I was then over seventeen years old.

At Winchester, I was placed in the Lower Sixth Form, where most of the girls were expected to enter one of the Oxford universities and were preparing for the entrance exams known as Responsions. The standard of learning was a great deal higher than I had been accustomed to, and even the German and French I had previously considered to be my best subjects fell far short of accepted standards. One of the required subjects was Anglo-Saxon.

Notices were put up on the board every Saturday evening listing church services which were to take place the following day at the Cathedral and two other parish churches, and names of those wishing to attend had to sign and state which place of worship they chose. Most elected to attend the Cathedral, where the music was beautiful and the service impressive, so visits there had to be rationed. As a nominal Protestant I dutifully attended one or other of them.

There were three boarding houses attached to the school, which was at the time situated in a rather dreary side street. Later, a fine new building was erected on the site of a games field at the top of a hill. The three school houses were called 'Venta', 'Caer Gwent' and 'Hyde Abbey'. I was allocated to the latter under the care of the house mistress, Miss Gregory. She was tall, regal, hard as flint and with a bitter and sarcastic tongue. She hated everything that savoured of popery. I suspected she may have been tipped off by my parents of my leanings towards Rome in the hope that she might be able to cure this rank heresy. It was probably how I landed up in Hyde Abbey. Whether it was so or not, life with her was a miserable affair. We clashed on every possible occasion and whenever I annoyed her as I frequently did, she would taunt me with thinking myself so religious and superior. I have no doubt that, being at a difficult age, I was obstreperous and argumentative and probably rubbed her up the wrong way more than necessary. I had acquired the habit at the convent of frequently crossing myself, and this action infuriated her still further. In retrospect I now sympathise with her. I was a spoilt child who needed a good spanking.

My two best friends at Hyde Abbey did not think much of my papist leanings either. One, Muriel Schoolbridge, was a staunch Protestant. The other friend was Nita Henson, but I do not think she subscribed to any particular church. She was exceedingly good at games and as the school largely modelled itself on Winchester College, prowess in sport was highly thought of. She was a clever girl and years later, during the Second World War attained high rank in the WRNS.

Autograph books were popular. As an instance of how I had not lost my talent for putting my foot in it, I said one day: "I wish I could get a real artist's or musician's or actor's signature – someone famous."

"Ask Nita's brother" chorused the girls, while Nita looked modestly down at her shoes.

"Oh I don't mean someone ordinary, I mean a well-known person" said I, and felt a bit silly when Leslie Henson arrived one afternoon to collect Nita.★

★(*Leslie Henson was well-known in his time as a comic actor. He had acted with Stanley Holloway and a young John Mills and was one of the founders of ENSA*).

When my year had elapsed, I left Winchester and returned home to celebrate the end of the war. Once home again, the first place I visited was the Convent, to see all my old friends, dear Madam Herminie and two special friends, Leila and Dorothy. My desire to become a nun had waned by this time, but I still wanted to become a Catholic. That would have to wait, I realised, until my parents gave their permission or until I was old enough to please myself.

Meanwhile I started to lead a social life which was not very productive career-wise but all that was expected of middle-class girls in the 1920s. Cecil and I attended classes once again (this time voluntarily) at the Misses Birds' establishment in order to learn all the latest steps in ballroom dancing. Mervyn, being much younger than us, was still at school in Dorset and therefore engaged in more serious studies.

Many friends of ours living around the town, all bright young things, joined the classes as well, and dancing became the highlight of the week. We also went to the silent films. Two picture theatres had just opened and also what were rather coyly called 'thés dansants' at the Polygon or South Western hotels. The Savoy Orphéans played the pops of the day – *Whispering, 'Sandman', Maggie, There's a Long Long Trail a-Winding*, etc, and we all had a great time. Leila Lewis, my great friend from schooldays who lived in Bath, came to stay with us and we would motor down to these dances in some rattletrap of a motor car, partly home-made I suspect and belonging to some boyfriend. They were real bone-shakers and great fun.

CHAPTER SEVEN

JACK

He was leaning against a wall between dances at Miss Bird's and my first glimpse was of a pair of nonchalantly-crossed trouser legs, as I was ascending the stairs. The next dance was about to begin and the young man to whom the legs belonged was introduced to me by Miss Bird as a prospective partner.

"Mr Holt," she said, and we took a turn round the floor. After a little while, he smiled at me and remarked: "By the way, my name isn't Holt, it's Locke." Holt or Locke, I did not really care very much. He was quite a good dancer for a beginner (for that was what he was), lithe on his feet and did not tread on mine. I was quite impressed. He was slim, had a pleasant speaking- voice and was not bad looking. We danced the next dance and all the rest for the remainder of the afternoon, trying not to notice Miss Bird's angry looks and requests to "change partners".

This was a Tuesday. On the Thursday of that week, Miss Bird was giving another lesson at a hall in Portswood, a Southampton suburb. He asked me to meet him there. It was an evening session and normally I was not allowed out at night. However, since he belonged to Miss Bird's classes and she was always most particular whom she accepted, whether children or adults, that was one hurdle overcome. His uncle was a Southampton solicitor, a firm known to my father, and so I was given permission to attend the class, provided I was in by a certain time.

I waited impatiently for Thursday evening and well before the hour we had arranged to meet, I was ready to catch a tram for Portswood Junction. Mr Locke was waiting for me at the Stag Gates, a familiar Southampton landmark now long gone, and my heart leapt when I saw him at the tram stop. We walked together to the hall, an unprepossessing place for a romantic rendezvous. It was defaced by innumerable war posters and ugly chipped brown paint and had been used for prisoners of war during the recent hostilities. Once again, we defied Miss Bird's orders to "please change partners" and danced together the whole evening.

We met frequently after that. He told me that after leaving school, his parents had arranged for him to be articled to his Uncle Alfred (the solicitor). He had unwillingly agreed to their wishes, but after some weeks in his uncle's firm he had decided he was unsuited to office life and signed on to join a sailing ship at a ridiculously low wage, undeterred by the prospect of harsh conditions and months away from home. His parents were naturally very disappointed with his decision. They could see no future in a life at sea, but Jack refused to change his mind, saving every penny of his meagre salary until he had repaid them the fifty pounds they had paid for his articles.

Life on sailing ships in the early part of the twentieth century was very hard. The meat they carried for crews' rations became so tainted that it had to be dragged through the sea to rid it of maggots. Jack once fell off the rigging in Arctic conditions and broke his hand. With no doctor on board, the method of setting the bones and pulling them into shape again was to force the patient to carry heavy buckets of coal around. There was no security of employment. Once back on shore, there was no guarantee that a crew would be taken on for another voyage.

By the time we met, he had progressed from sail to steam and life had become easier, with better pay and living conditions. But having satisfied his lust for travel and adventure – he had been round Cape Horn twice under sail – he was now beginning to wish he had acceded to his parents' wishes and pursued a shore job after all. The lure of sea life was beginning to pall, and being a little older he could now see the attractions of a warm comfortable office, a job with eventual status and prospects of promotion. He had made his choice and being the proud man he was, felt he must abide by it.

A big charity ball was to be held at the South Western Hotel and Jack had mentioned he might attend it. Naturally, I wanted to go too, and a kind godfather of mine, Mr Henry Glasspool, no longer young but nevertheless an extremely sprightly gentleman, knowing how badly I wanted to attend, asked my father if he could escort me to the dance. His wife Hetty was too delicate for such capers and did not care for dancing. Henry had been a pupil of Miss Bird (I think the whole town had at one time or another) and loved dancing. My father agreed and I was overjoyed. The friendship between Jack and myself had not advanced to the point where we automatically accompanied each other to every social occasion, but by that time, I knew I was in love with him.

The ball was to be quite an auspicious occasion with plenty of grand people there, and my mother set about buying me a new dress, cloak, shoes and stockings so that I could look my best and do credit to the family. On the evening of the dance, Henry called for me at 7.30 in a cab. Dressed in all my finery, I did feel that I was really looking my best and prayed that Jack would be there. It was by no means certain that he could manage it, as his next voyage was nearly due and he could be off again any day. As soon as we entered the ballroom, I looked eagerly around for him but he was nowhere to be seen. Assuming he had been unable to make it after all, it was with a heavy heart that I stepped out on the floor for the first dance with Henry Glasspool.

We were passing the entrance for the third time when I saw him. He was with Phyllis Faulkner. Not having a great deal of self-confidence, I could not conceive how anyone, knowing both Phyllis and me, could possibly prefer me to her. She had a very pretty pert little face and curly chestnut hair. I had to admit she was a lot better-looking than I was.

She and her brother Roy lived with their widowed mother in Carlton Crescent. Her family, Jack's and ours were mutual friends. When I discovered Jack knew her well, it worried me exceedingly and when I saw them together at the dance it was a bitter blow. Evidently, he was smitten with her, I told myself. I must eventually concede defeat and try to forget him if I could. When we passed on the dance floor, he with Phyllis, I with Henry, I looked the other way and ignored his smile of recognition.

The dance ended and Henry led me to a chair at the side of the room. "May I get you a lemonade, Kathleen?" he asked (alcoholic drinks were strictly forbidden to young ladies of my generation). I thanked him and he went off in the direction of the bar. Then I saw Jack hurrying over. He looked very debonair in his white tie and tails and my heart started thumping again. "Let me have the next dance," he whispered urgently. "I have something important to say to you. Please say yes."

"Oh dear," I thought. "This is the crunch. He is going to tell me he wants Phyllis and our friendship is at an end." As casually as I could sound although the words nearly stuck in my throat, I replied: "What about Phyllis? Don't you want to dance with her?"

"No" he said. "It is you I want to dance with. Please say yes."

Henry returned with the lemonade. "Don't you two worry about me," he said. "I've met several of my pals in the bar and have asked one or two of the wives for a dance, so Kathleen, if you want to join the younger set, go ahead. I'll come over from time to time to see how you are getting on." With that, he winked hugely at us both, smiled and departed. Dear kind considerate Henry. What a lot I owe him for that evening and come to think of it, what a lot I owe to Miss Bird (that most unlikely of Cupids) for having brought Jack and me together.

The band struck up a slow foxtrot. By the end of it, the glittering ballroom was transformed into a fairyland of lights, sweet music and whirling figures. We were dancing on air, our feet not touching the ground, two figures in a world of our own as only those who have experienced the ecstasy of being in love know.

When the first exaltations were over and we had come down to earth a little, Jack got down to practicalities.

"I'll be leaving England soon. It may be some time before we can get married. I have been offered a job in China with a company called Butterfield and Swire. It is a good one with chances of promotion and while out there, I'll be able to get my Master's Certificate."

Then came the bombshell. The job, he said, was for three years. We spent the rest of the evening in each other's company talking the sort of talk and using the sort of phrases lovers have spoken since time immemorial. I danced once or twice with Henry, who shrewdly noticed how the land lay. "Thought you two were a bit partial to each other," he remarked in his quaint old-fashioned way.

Sitting in the darkened alcove under the stairs, Jack and I kissed for the first time.

Jack had only a short time left before his embarkation, and it was unfortunate that it was just at this time I had to leave him for a few days to take a belated matriculation exam in London. I went with a cousin, Frances Ince, and we stayed at Streatham Hill with relations of my mother, the Colyers. Frank Colyer,* a doctor, was knighted for work done in the 1914/18 war treating the horrific injuries to jawbones sustained in the trenches from shell bursts. He was the brother of the Doctor Stanley Colyer I had been so fond of as a child. Frances was terribly nervous about the exams, but so elated was I after Jack's recent declaration of love that I sailed through the ordeal without a tremor. While in London, I received my first letter from him confirming his feelings for me. It was beautifully written, very poetic and I read and reread it dozens of times. In the end, it fell to pieces after being handled so much, but I kept the pieces!

Note: Sir Frank Colyer was a second cousin. His parents were James Colyer, born 1843, and Rebecca Hastings Farrow, born 1842. Rebecca was aunt to my grandmother, Violet Hastings Ince. Sir Frank was both a qualified doctor and dentist. He was a remarkable man. During the first world war, he served as consulting dental surgeon to the Croydon War Hospital and the Ministry of Pensions and his work done on the injuries to soldiers in the trenches earned him a KBE. Just before his death in 1954, a gold medal was struck for research and discoveries called the Colyer Medal and in America, the Colyer Institute was named after him. So he was quite a famous relation.

Jack met me at the station on my return and we went for a long walk on the common. We said little to one another but were just glad to be in each other's company and on the way back, we rested on a wooden bench overlooking one of the lakes, which was sparkling in the evening sunshine. We talked of getting married and with luck and he with a shore job, perhaps never parting again. The remainder of his leave was spent walking on the common or on the pier watching the ships, one of which was to bear him away from me very soon.

Being only nineteen, I was considered too young to become engaged to a chap who was to leave England so soon for three years. We exchanged photographs. I had a coloured one framed in velvet and another in sepia showing him in the uniform of a Third Officer. He left me his walking stick to look after until his return and to remember him by. Even young men used walking sticks then. We bade farewell at Southampton Station as his ship, one of the Blue Funnel Line, was sailing from Liverpool and I prepared myself for a long lonely wait.

After he left, there followed a hectic year from November 1920 to the end of 1921, during which my father, having served as sheriff for twelve months, became mayor. Although it was a strenuous and extremely busy time, I think he enjoyed every minute of his tenure. Not so my poor mother. She was expected to accompany him to nearly every civic event. Her speeches filled us all with dismay for she was not only very nervous but one of the world's worst speakers. Fortunately, since the audience was usually largely male and she was young and good-looking, her shortcomings were overlooked.

I attended many of the functions with my parents, and this helped to soften the effect of Jack's long absence. I was very glad of the distraction afforded, with perhaps the exception of the initial mayoral banquet, at which an ageing brigadier gave in his speech what seemed the entire history of the British Army. Everyone thought they were there for the night!

Other memorable occasions I greatly enjoyed. One was the visit of Prince Hirohito of Japan. The war with Japan was then many years into the future. We were invited to lunch on board his warship and the invitation was worded thus: "to Mr Mayor, Mrs Mayor and Miss Mayor". I very much liked being Miss Mayor, it sounded so grand. We were introduced to the strong rice wine saki at the luncheon, but thought it probably an acquired taste.

Another unforgettable event was the arrival of Charlie Chaplin. From modest beginnings, Chaplin had in ten years become very famous indeed and his return to his home town in London was looked forward to so much that huge crowds were waiting to greet him at Waterloo Station. But first, he had to run the gamut of his admirers in Southampton. In his autobiography, a local newspaper reports: "The 'Olympic' was fog-bound outside Southampton tonight and in the city there waited a huge army of worshippers come to welcome the little comedian. The police were busy making special arrangements to handle the crowd at the docks and at the civic ceremony in which Charlie is to be received by the Mayor." Chaplin wrote: "I was not prepared for this kind of welcome. Wonderful and extraordinary as it was, I would have postponed my visit until I felt more equal to it." Poor Chaplin, a modest and retiring man despite his fame, had been warned he would be mobbed on his arrival at Waterloo Station, but was not initially aware he had to get through the crush of admirers in Southampton first.

Our family were all tremendous fans. We were all introduced to him, and he must have wondered how many more Blatches he was going to meet! There was some criticism from council members that 'so august' a person as the Mayor should extend such an official welcome to a mere film star when these occasions should be reserved for royalty and other such dignitaries, but we did not care. After all, Charlie Chaplin's name is still remembered when other so-called more important people have long been forgotten. It was a very exciting day for the Blatch family.

My father, not a strong man, began to feel the journey from Westbourne Crescent to his office in Portland Terrace was proving too tiring. Besides, his many commitments at council meetings and other activities were mostly sited in the town centre, where Portland Terrace was very conveniently situated. So he and my mother turned the two top floors of the building into a family residence, and we moved there in due course. From the back of the house, there were lovely views over the Western Shore and the Solent to Marchwood beyond. From there, my mother and I had watched the ill-fated *Titanic* set out on her maiden and only voyage. The street was not then a through road, and with the Echo Office building blocking any further exit, there was no traffic at all. It was so quiet that the only noise at night came from courting felines in the street below.

I continued with a full social life, meeting friends and going to parties, but missed Jack a good deal. He wrote regularly, wonderful letters, describing the interesting places he had visited, journeys up the Yangtse Kiang River with the ever-present danger from pirates, the delights of Penang and Kowloon and the parties he attended in Hong Kong and Shanghai. When he had been away for about eighteen months, he decided that China was becoming too disturbed for him to consider remaining after his three-year contract had ended, so I lost my chance of ever seeing that fascinating country.

Then he wrote to say he thought it was time we got engaged and if I agreed, he would ask his mother to take me to a jeweller in the town to choose a ring. This plan I found a bit embarrassing. What if I chose something too expensive? In the end, with Mrs Locke's encouragement, it was agreed. I selected a diamond and sapphire half hoop, put it on my finger and became engaged by proxy.

The following summer, my parents, two brothers and I spent a holiday at St Malo in Brittany. For the first time in two and a half years I had not heard from Jack for some weeks and was getting anxious. My father was more annoyed than worried and lectured me more than once on getting engaged in such an unorthodox way. He was sure that Jack had found someone else and that sooner or later, I was going to get very hurt. But he had reckoned without the character of my fiancé, who even for those days, held old-fashioned views on the correctness of conduct. Woe betide anyone who deviated from society's rules, and those that broke them were definitely beyond the pale. To me, he was the very rock of steadfastness. I knew him and I knew I could trust him. Jack would never let me down.

St Malo was a picturesque old town but somewhat smelly owing to the many public conveniences at every street corner. The legs below the iron enclosures proved a slight distraction from the otherwise scenic beauties and were a source of much amusement on the part of my two brothers. But we enjoyed the holiday immensely. It was a lovely area with the Channel spreading out from the old walls surrounding the town, the surface broken here and there by small islands. One of the largest was called 'Isle de Seize Ombres' because of the flickering shadows over its bare rock.

After three weeks exploring Brittany we returned home, where I found a belated letter from Jack. It had been readdressed, which was why it had been delayed. He had been through a worrying time, having invested his savings in a school of languages promoted by a friend of his. The project folded and they both lost a fair amount of money with no hope of recovery.

The news was not as devastating to me as it was to him. I was just thankful and relieved to have heard from him at last. It did not matter if, because of his bad luck, our wedding might have to be postponed. His time abroad was nearly up and soon we would be together again. To me that was all that mattered. I carried the letter around with me reading it over and over again whenever I had a moment to myself, hugging the thought that I would soon be seeing him again.

My father was not so elated. He had hoped, I think, that the affair would fizzle out, as he considered Jack as a sailor would not make a suitable husband and that I would often lead a lonely life while he was away. But at long last Jack was home again and we knew that there would never be anyone else for either of us. My parents made the best of it and preparations for our wedding in the summer of 1923 went ahead.

CHAPTER EIGHT
A SAILOR'S WIFE

Jack had obtained his Master's Certificate in China, and after an interview in Liverpool he was accepted by the Cunard White Star Line as First Officer. My father offered to buy us a house after we were married, but since Jack would only be home for about fifty days in the year, I thought it best to remain for the present with my parents in Portland Terrace. It was very foolish of me to turn down such an offer. I would give a great deal for the same chance today.

The weather was dreadful on September 4th, our wedding day. Rain teemed down without a break from early morning to six o'clock in the evening. My mother, my friend Leila and I had made all the trousseau by hand. Since dress material was ridiculously cheap, it was the usual thing to do, if you made a mistake in cutting out, to simply discard the pieces and start again. I chose grey crêpe de chine for my wedding dress, with small pleats round the skirt, a cloche hat (very fashionable) and grey shoes and stockings to match. It sounds a funny colour to be married in but I considered it suited me better than white, which I thought too ordinary and conventional. Also, it was an economical outfit, since I wore it for going away in. We were married at the Church of All Saints, Below Bar, Southampton. Sadly, it is now a ruin, bombed and set on fire during the Second World War.

Our honeymoon travel to London was in style in a first-class railway carriage seen off by a crowd of relatives and friends. My father had arranged a programme of events for those invited to the wedding, a cricket match - fathers versus sons - in the afternoon (weather permitting) and in the evening seats were booked at the local cinema for a showing of *The Prisoner of Zenda*. By this time of course, Jack and I had arrived in London where he had booked a week's stay for us at the Strand Palace Hotel.

It was a good thing we travelled first class. We were in our wedding finery with confetti lying all over the seats and floor and were feeling very self-conscious. In the hotel lobby with the register in front of me, I asked what name I should sign. Whoops! Another faux pas! But of course the hotel staff knew we had just got married and were not there for an illicit stay (I hope).

We returned to Portland Terrace on September 11th and two days later, Jack sailed for New York on the *Mauretania*. He would come back on average every fortnight for two or three days' leave, which passed all too quickly, and after a hurried breakfast, would be back at the Docks again to rejoin his ship.

Early in November, I discovered to my joy that I was expecting a baby. Pregnancy then was looked upon as a sort of illness. Women did not do as much as they do nowadays and my usual energetic way of life was reined in somewhat. Morning sickness also took its toll. To while away the time, my father taught me to play auction bridge and solo whist, two games I have always loved. He also tried to teach my mother, but she had no card sense whatever. Her talents lay in more active sports like lawn tennis and ice skating and she excelled at both, even gaining a bronze medal for skating when she was in her fifties. Southampton was lucky in possessing a marvellous ice rink where international championships were often held. Sadly that too has gone, victim of the war.

For the birth of Shelagh Margaret in July, I went to a small nursing home in Hill Lane. Her father was away at the time and received the news by cable. Shelagh and I remained in the nursing home for a fortnight, during which time I crocheted myself a dress in mauve silk yarn, copying the lace design on the net curtains at the window.

Because she had always loved children, my mother took over the care of the baby after I came back home. She would come up every morning to give Shelagh her first bottle of the day and did all her washing for me. She used to worry a good deal about my father, who naturally was getting older. He also seemed to get tired easily, but nothing she could say would make him give up his Rotary Club or the demands of the Council Health Committee, all of which activities were voluntary, to say nothing of the work connected with his own profession. Now the strain and long hours were beginning to tell.

My mother liked a good game of tennis at weekends, and armed with two racquets she would set off for her club at Highfield. On Saturday, when she had gone to her club as usual, my father and I arranged to go on a coach trip to Winchester. As I had by now found a reliable baby sitter, my mother thought it might do him good as for the past week, he had complained of nagging pains in his chest. At the last moment however, the weather turned cold so we decided to put off our trip until the following week. Instead, my father left the house after lunch to call on one of his colleagues in the town.

At about teatime, I was rather surprised to hear someone calling up from the well of the hall in a feeble trembling voice. Neither of my parents were expected back before six o'clock. Cecil was in his room and I was not anticipating visitors on a Saturday afternoon. I ran downstairs to find my father supporting himself by clutching the banisters and obviously in great pain. I shouted for Cecil and together we managed to get him upstairs onto the bed, where he lay grey-faced and unable to speak.

From the downstairs office, I immediately phoned our doctor, only to find he was away for the day. I tried others but they were reluctant to attend another's patient. I finally managed to contact one who said that if our own doctor was still unavailable, he would attend. Cecil meanwhile rang the tennis club from a nearby call-box to alert my mother. She dropped her racquets there and then and rushed home in a taxi, arriving at the same time as the doctor.

My father was given a pain-killing drug which seemed to ease him and help his difficult breathing and shortly afterwards, he fell peacefully asleep. We were told to keep him absolutely quiet and the doctor said he would call again last thing that night to see how he was getting on. We were all terribly worried and sat around silently all the rest of that evening while my mother never left his bedside. As there seemed nothing else we could usefully do, Cecil and I eventually went up to our rooms and fell asleep exhausted.

The following morning, my mother came to help me as usual with the baby. She looked terribly tired and pale and her eyes were red with weeping. She said that at midnight my father had died in her arms. There was nothing I could say or do to comfort her. Neither of them were very old. They had loved one another so much. Disagreements had been rare and they had enjoyed a supremely happy marriage. It was dreadfully tragic that it had to end when they were both comparatively young. He died on the 14th October, her forty-seventh birthday.

The next year, I found I was having another baby. The pregnancy was most distressing and I suffered from morning sickness throughout the nine months. The baby turned out to be another girl, and she died soon after birth. Jack brought Shelagh in to see me and he tried to be comforting, but in a rather clumsy way. "We don't really mind since it was just another girl, do we?" was not the most diplomatic remark he could have made, and it did not lessen the disappointment. The child's fontanel at the top of the head was unusually wide and nothing could be done. At the very best, she could only have survived a few days.

I asked the doctor about subsequent children. "How do I know I won't have another like her?" I asked. "About as likely as dealing yourself thirteen trumps at bridge" was his reply.

Jack and I had both wanted a boy and in 1927, our son, John David Ivor, was born. This time everything went smoothly from start to finish and I felt wonderful when he was put into my arms for the first time. Our little boy was here at last and fit and healthy. We were both delighted. He was a pretty child, chubby and rosy-faced, and attracted a lot of attention on our walks. Like Cecil when he was young, he smiled at all and sundry and was a very friendly baby.

When Jack was about two, I used to take him to Hampshire Cricket Ground. My father had loved the game and it rubbed off on me. But a lively two-year old was not perhaps the best companion. He used to wander off looking for something more exciting than a lot of fellows hitting a ball about and discovered a new, more interesting game. When the male spectators were concentrating on a particularly tense part of the match, sitting forward on the wooden benches in order not to miss a single stroke, John would be quietly taking packets of cigarettes from their back trouser pockets. I was very embarrassed when this budding Fagin proudly presented me with his booty and had to go around seeking the rightful owners, if I could find them. Fortunately, they took it in good part and John was given some sweets in return for the cigarettes.

Through the 1930s life for us was fairly uneventful, except for one important happening. My daughter had been enrolled at the Convent at the age of four and a half and John also went there, as boys were accepted up to the age of seven. Were they thinking perhaps of the dictum of the Jesuits? After my father's death, my mother became rather lost for interests. She never got over the shock of his sudden death and now it was her turn to have leanings towards the Church of Rome. She had become great friends with Sister Mary Oswald, a very large jovial Irish lady, and the two of them would enjoy huge jokes together. So it was my mother more than I who eventually propelled us all in the direction of Catholicism and in 1933 we were received into the Church. At about the same time Jack was baptised a Catholic by a priest in New York.★

★*I am never sure that Dad was all that enthusiastic about religion in general. He was something of a pragmatist and hated over-sentimentality of any kind, but I suppose he went along with the trend for the sake of peace. Needless to say, my brother John and I had no choice in the matter. My paternal grandparents were staunch Protestants and were so shocked by our decision to become Catholics, they refused to speak or to have any contact with us for some time, but family ties were too strong and they eventually became reconciled to the situation.*
Shelagh

For the four of us back in England there was a 'wedding breakfast' at the Convent, after which we duly made our first confessions. It had taken a long time to come to this decision. I had wanted to have the children baptised Catholics just after they were born and had tentatively broached the subject with my old form mistress, Madam Imelda, but she poured cold water on the idea immediately, pointing out that, since the rest of the family were not Catholic, it was not appropriate. So I deferred action for the time being and we all continued to attend St Mary's C of E church on Sundays.

My two brothers had long since gone their own ways. Cecil was now a fully-fledged solicitor and had obtained a post with Messrs. Julius and Creasy in Sri Lanka (then called Ceylon). He was now married. My younger brother Mervyn worked for the Shell Oil Company in London. He loved motoring and would often come down to Southampton to take us all out in his Delage for outings and picnics in the New Forest. The two children would travel in the dicky, where they spent much of the time quarrelling, and when he was home, they would get their due deserts from their father, who rightly would stand none of it. However, the grown-ups enjoyed bowling along the then empty roads of the Forest, wind in their hair, savouring the sweet sounds and scents of unspoiled countryside. They were marvellous days.

Because of the General Strike and the Depression, Jack and I were no better off than when he had first joined the Cunard, and when the children came along, money was tight. We did still manage the occasional summer holiday in the Isle of Wight, but sadly never together, as he was not able to get more than a few days' leave at a time, and that not very often. My father's houses had been sold by then and it was a boarding house stay for us. He had been right. It was a lonely existence being a sailor's wife, but I never regretted marrying Jack.

Being able to see his family so seldom, Jack had become thoroughly disillusioned with the sea by this time and made two abortive attempts to get himself a shore job, firstly, at Trinity House ("too young and inexperienced"), secondly, with the Port of London Authority, where someone else's qualifications were considered superior.

By the time our third child came along in 1936 - Francis - we decided he was to be the last, as three were all we could afford. By that time, we had moved from Portland Terrace to a home of our own, a semi-detached in Blenheim Avenue at the top of The Avenue (the broad highway that leads into the heart of Southampton) and we let the top part of the house to help pay the mortgage.

My mother, still living at Portland Terrace, also decided to take tenants. Her late husband's generosity to some of his poorer clients had not left her a great deal to live on and she did not relish being alone in a large house of four storeys and a basement. The ground and first floors were still occupied by a solicitor's office. We had formerly lived on the top floor and this she now let to a middle-aged lady who, like herself, was a widow. They got on famously. My mother moved to the next floor down and made a nice flat for herself. It had a glass-covered verandah at the back with a stunning view over the Solent, and this she converted into two long narrow rooms, one a kitchenette, the other a little bedroom with the main room opening onto the verandah, used as a sitting room. Overlooking Portland Terrace at the front were a second bedroom and large bathroom. Altogether, a comfortable residence and room for the family if they wanted to stay.

Years before, at the time of my father's death, poor Marie Bernigaud was recovering from a road accident she had suffered. My mother, not long after she was widowed, went over to Paris to see Marie, who was delighted to meet her old friend again, and they spent the week of her stay reminiscing. The visit helped both of them - Marie's recovery and my mother's sense of bereavement and unaccustomed loneliness.

When the tenant at Portland Terrace left to remarry, her place was taken by a very nice Anglo-Indian couple. One terrible night, after too hot a bath, the husband leaned against the balustrade fronting the stairs, felt giddy, overbalanced and fell the full length through the well of the house. This must have been forty feet or more. Of course, nothing could be done for him and it affected us deeply. For a long time afterwards, there were no more tenants.

Chapter Nine

War

1936 was a year of crisis on the national and international scene. King Edward VIII abdicated to marry Mrs Simpson. Germany re-occupied the Rhineland and Churchill demanded rearmament of British forces. The next three years were decidedly jittery and the construction of air raid shelters in the Avenue and elsewhere in Southampton pointed to the possibility of another war with Germany. We heard that Southampton might be a major target for air attacks in the event of hostilities, so I shut up the house in Blenheim Avenue and at her invitation, decamped with the three children to my great friend in Bath, Leila Lewis, since married and now Leila Emerson. In sombre mood we sat round the wireless set in Leila's sitting room and listened to the declaration of war against Germany announced by Neville Chamberlain.

Leila's family home, long sold and now turned into a hotel, stood on one of the hills surrounding Bath City. Three generations lived there, Leila, her husband Ron and their three daughters, Nesta her sister and husband Bill, with their three daughters and small son and Leila's elderly parents. Fortunately, being a large house, and even with so big a family, there was still room to spare. The family business founded by Leila's parents, a newsagent and tobacconist in the centre of the city, was run by the whole family apart from the young children, a good and profitable arrangement and they all seemed to get on so well together.

They were an extremely kind and hospitable family and even though it must sometimes have been a strain having four, sometimes five extra people to cater for, they never appeared to mind one bit. In fact, I really believed they enjoyed the company and we most certainly did. Leila and I had always been the best of friends over many years, and the rest of her family were as charming and nice as herself.

We obviously could not impose on their hospitality too long, so the children and I (Jack was now back with his ship) took temporary lodgings in a cottage at Peasdown just outside Bath and then at Lansdown on the western side. Both of the old cottages were very dilapidated and in one, the bed disappeared through the floor! In another, which was part of a farm, Francis was found in the bull's pen stroking the animal's nose while it calmly went on eating. He could not understand what the panic was all about - "it was a nice cow."

Jack had for years signed up to the Royal Naval Reserve and had attended courses at Portsmouth and Plymouth. Now the time had come for him to be called up. While he awaited orders, we rented a new bungalow built in the garden of a retired bank manager at Limpley Stoke, a few miles outside Bath. It had the most spectacular views across the valley to the wooded hills opposite. At the time we moved in late autumn, the hills around were ablaze with gold and russet. Far below us (we were about 500 feet up) the little train that ran from Bath to Bradford-on-Avon puffed its way alongside the Kennet and Avon Canal, lazily winding its way through the wooded slopes. It was a most beautiful spot.

Not quite so beautiful was the climb down the hill to the village and the station. It would have tested the skill of the most ardent mountaineer and it was a good thing we were young and agile. Getting back up was even worse. That winter (1939/40) was one of the hardest the country had known. Snow and frost lasted for weeks. The main cable of our all-electric bungalow was attached to our landlord's chimney and the ice around it daily grew thicker until one night, the whole lot came crashing down, chimney and all. We were left with no heat, no light nor anything to cook by and only a small fire in the sitting room to warm the entire house. The walls of the bungalow had never properly dried out and long icicles hung both inside and outside the bedroom and bathroom walls. Then we all went down with flu, but even the doctor could not make it up the steep hillside in her car.

The winter had its compensations - at least for Shelagh. My mother had taught her to ice-skate and she took the opportunity of the conditions to skate along the frozen canal as far as Bradford-on-Avon and back again. She declared it a most wonderful and uplifting experience and utterly peaceful. Thick woods lined the water's edge the whole way and not a sound to be heard except that of her skates on the thick ice, and a good thing it was. I am not sure we knew of the expedition beforehand, but if she had disappeared through the ice, I doubt whether we would have ever known what happened! She and John were now back at school, Shelagh a weekly boarder at Bath Convent, John a full boarder at Prior Park College, an establishment run by the Christian Brothers.

I returned to Hampshire in the late spring, leaving both children as boarders in Bath, and rented a house in the heart of the New Forest at Linwood, belonging to a young doctor and his wife who were shortly leaving for Palestine. Although a modern house, there were no less than eight acres of wild forest and heathland attached. When the children came for the summer holidays, they discovered that we actually 'owned' a tennis court, very overgrown in the middle of a wood, and a grey forest pony annexed one of the outhouses. It used to wander in on cold nights and bed itself down. At various times we saw foxes, badgers, adders, rabbits and hares in front of our windows, a veritable paradise for a naturalist. John was a keen butterfly enthusiast and made firm friends with a very old man living alone in the heart of the forest who was also a keen lepidopterist. The two would discuss the butterfly world for hours and John eventually ended up with a wonderful collection of both foreign and British butterflies, and in those days, there was no better place than the New Forest to study them.

The war had not, up to then, been very evident. One afternoon I took a deckchair into our wild garden for a rest. It was a warm sunny afternoon, no sound but the hum of bees and it was all delightfully peaceful. Dozing a little, I thought how lovely it would be to open my eyes and find someone beside me with a telegram from Jack to say he was coming home on leave. Hearing a slight rustle, I opened my eyes to see a little girl from the post office with, in her hand, a telegram. It was from Jack telling me he was coming home on leave!

He spent a week with me and said he had been

allocated to a ship of his own line (Cunard) converted from a passenger liner to a troopship. He was to be sent to an unknown destination but had been ordered to take his 'whites' (tropical gear) with him. We assumed therefore that the "unknown destination" would be somewhere in the Far or Middle East.

After he had left and when all seemed quiet again, we were 'commandeered' by the Army. Hanging out some washing one day I heard the noise of car engines, a most unusual sound in that part of the Forest, and was surprised to see a group of soldiers standing around a couple of military vehicles with what looked like long tubes protruding from the back. An officer approached and told me he was in charge of an aircraft early warning system. The tubes were to pick up the first far-off sound of approaching enemy planes, and they would have to be placed in our garden. He apologised but explained that as it was wartime, civilians would have to comply with military requirements.

I was then asked, since houses were few and far between in that part of the Forest (we were literally miles from anywhere), if I could supply water and baths for his men. I had no option but to agree to his request.

The engines for the equipment to detect aircraft would start up in the middle of the night, sounding like giant vacuum cleaners, and would scare me to death, for they gave the impression that the whole of the German Luftwaffe must be approaching. Sometimes, the soldiers would ring the doorbell in the middle of the night or later, asking to be allowed to telephone headquarters. It was not the most comfortable time to find oneself in the middle of a potential battlefield. Once again (it was holiday time), it was mainly Shelagh who enjoyed the situation as she admiringly watched the manoeuvres of the British Tank Corps as they trundled through our garden! John was too busy catching butterflies to bother with military matters.

Towards the end of the summer, some friends of our relations in the States invited us to stay with them in America. Since it looked as if it would be some time before I saw Jack again, I decided to accept their kind invitation. Our house in Blenheim Avenue had by that time been sold and we were free from encumbrances. Our friends in America had written to say they wanted to help the war effort and by extending hospitality to a British family, they thought this would be one way of doing it. How could I refuse so generous an offer?

We left Liverpool Docks on a cold grey day, my mother accompanying us to see us off and wish us bon voyage. As I watched her figure grow smaller and smaller on the quayside, I wondered if we would see her again. The future looked so uncertain. It seemed sensible to be taking the children out of England at such a time but perhaps hostilities would soon be over and before long, we would be on our way home again.

It was a rough voyage, which was fortunate since such weather curtailed U-boat activity. The captain of our ship, the *Antonia*, was a friend of Jack's and after a few days, he asked me to his cabin for a drink. I was feeling too seasick at the time and it was not until nearing the end of the journey that I was able to accept his invitation. Still queasy and a bit unsteady on my feet, I eventually found my way to his cabin and knocked weakly.

He was most welcoming, and this cheered me up somewhat. I told him Jack had gone abroad somewhere, but I had no idea exactly where. When drinks had been poured I remarked: "I've heard we are not going to Montreal after all, but to Halifax."

"Who says we are going to Halifax?" he retorted, almost angrily. I knew better than to press the matter. Montreal, Halifax, I knew neither place. It would just be nice to see land again.

The rumours had been correct and we eventually steamed into Halifax Harbour. There were several ships at anchor, all heavily camouflaged. One had a distinctly familiar appearance. I looked around for the First Officer who had just passed me on deck and pointed out this particular vessel.

"What ship is that over there?" I asked him. "It looks like a Cunarder".

"It is" he replied. "It…" – he looked hard at the subject of our discussion – "It's either the *Laconia,* the *Aurania* or the *Franconia*. I can't be sure but I can find out for you." I wondered then if another miracle like the telegram was about to occur.

Presently he returned. "It is the *Aurania*" he said with a smile "and I understand your husband is on her. You might like to write a note to him and the tender will take it over."

The miracle had happened. Here were we, quite by chance in the same port, with me thinking he had gone to the other end of the world and him thinking I was still in the New Forest! My note duly went over on the tender and in a little while it returned, with my Jack on board.

He was as amazed as we were. Seeing his entire family standing at the rails of the *Antonia* waving frantically was indeed an unexpected sight, particularly as we were all reconciled to the prospect of not seeing him again for months, perhaps years. The captain of his ship had generously given him three days' leave, so after the initial fond greetings, we set off to find digs in the town. Finding lodgings in a hurry for five of us was not easy, but the wife of the owner of a small restaurant where we had supper put us on to a friend of hers who had two spare rooms to let and sufficient beds to go round.

In all the excitement, I had completely forgotten to let our hosts in Philadelphia know that we were going to be delayed. They were rather annoyed at this as they had been notified by the Cunard of our ship's arrival and were expecting us the following day. I remembered only the evening of our final departure from Halifax to wire them and felt dreadfully guilty at this oversight. It was an unforgiveable breach of courtesy and I can offer no excuse except that my mind was in a whirl and I could not have been thinking straight.

Once more, Jack and I parted in anxious circumstances, but this time, there was a tacit understanding that if his ship continued to be based at Halifax, after spending a reasonable time in the States, we would return there. I would be able to receive the Admiralty allotment of pay and he could come to us whenever the *Aurania* was in port.

Our poor, patient hosts in Philadelphia had postponed a holiday in Miami to greet us, but left soon after. They had a wonderful Japanese cook called Nishi who stayed behind to look after us and a friend was allocated to show us round the city. The apartment in which we found ourselves consisted of six bedrooms, six bathrooms, two kitchens, a laundry room and a vast hall. We learned that domestic help in America was very difficult to get and terribly expensive, so carpets and chairs, when they got dirty, were simply sent away to be cleaned or replaced.

Our hosts, Mr and Mrs Funk, were very generous indeed. Although obviously wealthy people, they undertook to support us during our stay and educate the children, and they even provided us with a separate flat when they returned from holiday. We were provided with an allowance to live on and sometimes, they would help us out by taking us all to various foreign restaurants on Nishi's day off. Expensive restaurants too, and the food was always invariably good.

Shelagh was enrolled as an art student at the Curtis School of Music and Art recommended by our hosts, whose son Henry also attended the school. John and Francis went to a Quaker day school. John, then aged twelve, was completely bowled over by his new country. He reported back that all his school friends, from about the age of eight, actually drove themselves to school in their own motor cars.

Always good at science, about a week after we arrived, he spotted a poster in a shop window advertising a competition to solve a physics problem from a demonstration model in the window. "It seemed easy" he said afterwards, "so I just went in and gave them what I thought was the solution to the problem."

It turned out to be correct, and his prize was a trip by air over the city and a slot on local radio. He was now even more impressed. "It is so wonderful here," he announced over the radio. "Everything is much, much bigger and better than in England." This was just what the listeners wanted to hear and it went down very well.

He was not the only one impressed with Philadelphia. Besides being a beautiful city with its wide boulevards and marvellous parks, museums, public gardens and huge skyscraper apartment stores such as Wanamaker's, I had the unforgettable experience of attending a concert given by the great Rachmaninoff with Leopold Stokovsky conducting the Philadelphia Symphony Orchestra.

What an evening it was. Rachmaninoff played sixteen of his compositions in his faultless, fluid style without a note of a musical score. The hall was packed to the doors, the huge audience even forming a semi-circle on the stage itself. I had been lucky enough to obtain a ticket through two elderly ladies in the next flat to ours who had a spare ticket and gave it to me.

Before starting to play, the great man would lay his very white hands lightly on the keyboard, then slowly turn on the stool, look around the auditorium and pause. If among the audience there was the slightest sound or movement, he would wait motionless until one could literally hear a pin drop. Then - and only then - would he begin to play. What a showman! It had the desired effect, and stunned his audience into awe-inspired admiration.

A presidential election took place when we were in Philadelphia, the two main candidates being Franklin D. Roosevelt and Wendell Wilkie. We heard them both speak when they came to the city and found the campaign and all the razzmatazz very interesting and exciting. We favoured Roosevelt because he was so pro-British, but were warned by our hosts not to show open bias in public. This of course we would never have done anyway. Shelagh showed how neutral we were by buying rosettes of both parties and wearing them proudly on each lapel of her coat. As it happened of course, Roosevelt won, but both Roosevelt and Wilkie proved good friends to Britain in the later stages of the war.

Jack was still on convoy duty in and out of Halifax, so I decided it was time to say goodbye to our kind and generous patrons and make preparations to leave for Canada. Jack was at sea, but had managed to find us a semi-basement furnished flat near Halifax town centre so on arrival, we made for the address given. By this time, settling into new lodgings had become almost second nature and we quickly spread ourselves and various belongings over the three rooms. They were dark and rather dingy, a far cry from our Philadelphia flat, but at least we had a roof over our heads.

Halifax itself, in those wartime days, looked pretty run down. A town of mainly wooden buildings badly in need of a lick of paint, it was still recovering from the awful explosion during the 1914-18 war when a munitions ship in the harbour blew up, causing immense destruction to the town and heavy loss of life. While we were there, a bad epidemic of diphtheria was raging and everyone had to report for tests to see if they were susceptible to the disease. Fortunately, we were given the OK.

On his travels, Jack had met a Canadian Naval officer living with his family in a country district known as the North-West Arm. The 'Arm' was a sea inlet that stretched itself through the scrubby landscape where, in season after we went to live there, we were able to collect countless pounds of blueberries that grew wild on the heathland there, and come home laden for them to be turned into jams and pies. Jack's friend had recently been posted to Esquimalt in West Canada and he suggested we might like to take over their house during his absence.

Before moving however, we had to obtain permission from our landlady to terminate our tenancy agreement and re-let the flat. She rather grudgingly agreed and I placed an advertisement in the local paper. The response was truly staggering. There must have been a great housing shortage, because people started coming at 7.30 the next morning, not in ones and twos, but in groups. This went on all day until about 9 pm. It was impossible to keep track of them all, although Shelagh did her best to help. By late evening I realised I must have promised the flat to at least three different families, one of which belonged to the Canadian Mounted Police!

We thought at nine o'clock that must be the end of the applicants, but at 10pm there was another ring at the front door. Shelagh answered it and a man standing on the step offered her ten dollars if she could persuade her mother to let him have the apartment – sight unseen!

When the landlady heard of the scramble to get the flat, she was not too pleased. "If I'd known so many people wanted it I'd have let it myself," she grumbled (She meant of course at a higher rent). I did not argue. After all, we were lucky to have extricated ourselves so easily.

Our new house was built entirely of wood and probably a fire hazard, particularly as the inhabitants of the 'Arm' (as we now were), paid no rates as it was a sparsely-inhabited area and therefore could not summon the Fire Brigade. The house was warmed by two very large anthracite stoves and cooking was done on an ancient and ornate free-standing iron cooker. We felt very rural.

We shared a well for drinking water with a family who lived a few hundred yards away. They and we were practically the only people in that neck of the woods. The water was lovely, clear and icy cold, much better I thought than the mains water we had been used to.

One day, we lost our adopted cat, Pink Nose. I looked everywhere for poor Pink Nose and by the evening, came to the sad conclusion he must have fallen down the well which had a gap where the lid did not fit properly. I went to warn our neighbours, the Barrys, and advise them to boil the water until we had found our cat. Mrs Barry merely laughed at the suggestion and answered that they had frequently drawn up dead rats in the bucket. The odd cat hardly mattered. Sadly, we never found Pink Nose.

We were warned by the naval authorities against careless talk. Halifax was so important to the war effort and the Atlantic convoys upon which Britain depended and the U-boat activity was so pronounced at the time (1940/41), that it had become a hotbed of secret agents. I quite often overheard people discussing sailing dates and other such information in cafés and shops in the town, so any German spy must have had an easy time of it. More than once, Jack's captain visited us to ask if we had heard of anything because he had received evidence of a dangerous leakage of information in the town. During our discussions, I pointed out that as the cliff tops all around the harbour were open to the public, anyone with a pair of binoculars could watch the ships going in and out of the port with ease.

We spent about a year in Canada. Francis was still very young, but Shelagh and John enjoyed the new life. John was still butterfly collecting and had discovered interesting new species of butterflies and moths in the woods all around us. He was nothing if not resourceful, and when he found an old derelict rowing boat abandoned beside a large lake near the house, he patched it up with chewing gum! He even went on fishing expeditions with it and supplied us with some good dinners. But the fishing came to an abrupt end when one day he found the boat, moored by the bank, had sunk, chewing gum and all. We were thankful he was not in it at the time.

We gradually adapted to country living. There were no shops nearby, so Mrs Barry taught me how to make home-made bread, and although we had not quite got round to living on bear and moose, there were plenty of those not far away and I was beginning to feel like Ma Kettle. It was the usual hard Canadian winter and there were chipmunks busily burrowing into the wooden walls of the bathroom.

Quite early on, we had acquired two more cats. One had served his time on the submarine *Forth*, whether as stowaway or signed-on crew member I am not sure, but when he joined our ship, he was naturally given the name Forth. When the other cat came along, he was inevitably named Fifth. Forth was slightly independent and dignified, as befitted an ex-Royal Navy member. Fifth was all fluff, affection and playfulness. When we left Canada they were found good homes, but we missed them a lot.

After several months in Canada, we were informed that the Admiralty, no doubt unwilling to allow too many funds out of the country, decreed that naval allowances (allotments) would in future only be paid to those families who had come to Canada before June 1940. This meant we would be virtually penniless. I wrote at once to the authorities explaining our situation and in the meantime, was forced to borrow from friends to tide us over. Finally in desperation, I sent Shelagh to the pawnshop with my beautiful diamond and sapphire engagement ring, since the four of us still had to eat.

The following day, feeling somewhat depressed, I came home from doing some necessary shopping and flopped down in the nearest armchair. It was about lunchtime. I wearily reached out, switched on the wireless and was unprepared for the news announcement: "The German High Command announced early this morning that the *Aurania* had been torpedoed and sunk in convoy."

At first, numbed with shock as if in a dream, I went out of the house and walked down the lane I had so recently come up. A woman I knew stopped and spoke to me. She was the mother of a Canadian naval officer whose family lived not far away. I blurted out to her the news I had just heard. "Come in for a moment" she said. "Wally is home. He will have received the message. Perhaps things aren't as bad as you think."

I accompanied her to the house. Her son was in the sitting-room writing at his desk. "Yes it is true," he said, "the ship has been torpedoed, but not sunk. On the contrary, she is heading for home under her own steam and doing twelve knots." He looked pleased to have been the bearer of such welcome news. I of course was overjoyed, thanked them both and hurried back down the town to relay the news to other wives I knew who had husbands on the *Aurania*. The next afternoon, a cable arrived from Jack saying that the ship had arrived safely at their destination.★

★*Note: Lieut. CDr E.J. Binfield DSC, RD,RNR, on board the* Aurania *at the time, gave a graphic account of the action:*

"One night when we were some 600 miles from the coast of Ireland, found me as OOW of the Middle Watch. The night was very dark. Aurania *was the rear ship of the Port Column and it was with great difficulty that I could distinguish the next ahead and next abeam. At about 0220, when life seems at its lowest ebb, the Sub-Lieutenant of the Watch came up and told me that a message had just come through from the Admiralty giving the position of a German U-boat. I remarked to him, "That's just about where we are now, inform Father of the signal." He departed and I moved to the Port side of the bridge.*

A minute later, without any warning, a column of smoke and spray shot up to an enormous height from right under me. I wasn't conscious of any explosion, but I was very conscious of the fact that we had been hit in the for'ard magazine, and for a split second I waited for the world to disintegrate about me. It didn't. Automatically and without thinking, I went through the oft rehearsed drill of sounding off Action Stations, turning towards the enemy and easing the engines, seeking what protection I could whilst awaiting the fall of the multitude of fittings that had been flung up by the explosion. Then, like hail, baulks of timber, parts of rafts, and jagged pieces of metal crashed about me, plus tons of water. By miracle, nothing hit me, nor despite the fact that the bridge was flooded, did I even get wet. Our bridge, of course, was quite open, and except for a light covered rail, quite unprotected.

The ship listed immediately 20 degrees to Port, but reports fast pouring in were reassuring. No 3 Hold was wide open to the sea, and scores of drums were washing out. No. 2 was flooding, as were the Deep Tanks. But no more torpedoes had come our way, the engines were behaving perfectly, and the remaining underwater compartments with their packing of drums would provide ample flotation. With the flooding of the Deep Tanks the ship gradually returned to the upright and we proceeded on our way, well astern of the squadron, with one escort in attendance, rejoicing at 12 knots.

After the attack, whilst preparing the boats in case of necessity, through some accident one of the Port boats carried away, taking with it four members of the ship's company. Two were never seen or heard of again. A third was picked up by an escort. A few hours later we tuned into Hamburg and heard Lord Haw Haw *announce that HMS* Aurania, *laden with troops and sailing with a very fast convoy, had been torpedoed and sunk with all hands. "Sunk with all hands", "laden with troops" and "very fast convoy" made us suspect that our fourth involuntary absentee - an ex London postman with a vivid imagination - had been picked up by the U-boat and had 'spread himself'. Later we learned that this was indeed the case. Unfortunately some of the home papers published the Hamburg report, causing great distress among our next-of-kin.*

Two days later we steamed into Rothesay Bay, slightly down by the head, but otherwise looking remarkably sound."

(quotation by kind permission of the Cunard Archive, Liverpool University - ref: D42/PR3/16/19)

Further Note: The names of the two missing men were Leading Seaman George R. Brown and Able Seaman Victor A. Pancott. Gunner Charles Stewart, Able Seaman Cornelius O'Keefe and Able Seaman Abed Graves were picked up by HMS Croome (L62), but Bertie E. Shaw, who was taken prisoner by the U-boat crew, the "ex-London postman with the vivid imagination", is believed by many to have been the hero of the hour because he saved the ship from further attack by telling his captors it had been "sunk with all hands".

I heard afterwards that the ship had been torpedoed in the magazine, yet not a single shell had exploded. They were later detonated in the sea off Scotland and every one of them found to be alive! The ship had in any case been due for laying up for several months, possibly for good. Jack had known this before setting sail, but of course could divulge nothing of it to me. Not wishing to leave us stranded in a foreign country, he had introduced me to an English naval officer who he said would help us in the event of any difficulty while he was away. He further said "If ever you find that, for any reason, it is expedient to bring yourself and the children back home, telephone him, but for God's sake don't mention ships by name nor speak of convoys. Just say: 'what about the big movement?' and he will know what you mean and that you require a passage to England."

The time had come and I followed his instructions. "Four sailors will call at your house tomorrow morning – be ready" was the terse reply. It was common knowledge that convoys sailed from Halifax roughly every four weeks, so I surmised there must be one ready to put to sea almost immediately. I fetched Shelagh and John from their respective schools and we started to pack up and tidy the house for departure, it must be admitted, in some panic. I wrote to warn the owners that we would be leaving shortly.

Then, that afternoon, I heard from the Admiralty that they had paid no less than five months' allotment into our bank account. This created more panic. I phoned to thank them and ask that the sum be forthwith returned to its source in England. We found homes for the cats and the two older children and I rushed around like mad things, cleaning, tidying, shoving our belongings into any corner and space that could be found in our luggage and finally, everything was packed and labelled. Our departure had been so 'hush hush' I was not even able to go next door and say goodbye to Mrs Barry, which was a shame, since she had been a good friend, and I resolved to drop her a line on our return to England.

Francis, too young to be of much help, found a photo of Cecil (who then sported a moustache) among all the packing paraphernalia. He gazed at it for some while and then asked: "Did God make Hitler?" He said it in a manner that implied God must have slipped up somewhere.

"Yes, I expect so" said I, busy with other things.

"But why did God make Hitler?" I did not reply, being occupied with writing out labels.

"Humph!" he pondered "s'pose it's a military secret." To his mind, since everything else seemed to be a military secret, so that must be the answer, and he went off to bother one of his siblings.

There had been no time to retrieve my engagement ring, and I never saw it again. The three of us worked well into the night, the first really cold one of the winter. When in the early hours of the morning we lay down for a short rest, it was impossible to sleep. The stoves had all been let out and the bitter cold penetrated everywhere. After a sketchy breakfast at 6.30 am, punctually at 7.30 a Jeep and four sailors duly arrived to collect us and our belongings. An hour later, we were walking briskly up the gangway of the *Andes* (of the Royal Mail line, now converted into a troop ship).

CHAPTER TEN

ENGLAND AND SCOTLAND

Again the sea was rough, so there were no U-boats, but seasickness once again took its toll and laid us all low except Francis, who was taken care of for a couple of days by one of the kind nurses on board. The *Andes* docked at Liverpool, edging her way carefully through a forest of masts belonging to sunken ships littering the Mersey. A rumour went the rounds that there would almost certainly be an air-raid soon. There was nearly always one when a convoy arrived, but this time, it did not happen and I took the children for a meal at a nearby restaurant while we waited for a train to take us to Glasgow, as I had found out that Jack was based in Greenock.

A waiter at the restaurant, when asked where we could find some shops, as I needed one or two items we had forgotten to pack, replied gloomily: "No shops. All gone." The train was late in leaving and by the time we finally reached Glasgow, it was two hours behind time. By then, thoroughly out of sorts, in need of a wash and with children and luggage to cope with, I was not in the best of moods. We now had to catch a connection to Greenock, and it was now about midnight. Someone seemed to be standing in my way in the gloom of blackout. I was struggling with about ten suitcases, Shelagh was rounding up the boys and we all felt tired and dishevelled, and I looked up annoyed at this man, ready to deliver a sharp rebuke.

It was none other than Jack. He had come to Glasgow to meet us, and how glad I was to see him. During his long wait for the train, he had enlisted the help of the WVS (Women's Voluntary Service) and they had given him an address in Glasgow where we could all stay. We arrived by taxi at one am. An elderly lady opened the door and stared at us in some astonishment. "I was told to expect three little girls," she said "Obviously there has been a muddle somewhere. Come in anyway and I'll see what I can do."

Such kindness and hospitality at one in the morning! We even got hot baths at that late hour and a good supper into the bargain. Thank you, Glasgow. I shall always be grateful for that night of refreshing rest.

There was no chance of moving to Greenock, as the place was already overcrowded with service personnel, so after a search round the district, we found digs at Helensburgh, a pleasant little town just north of Dumbarton on the Gair Loch. At a vantage point nearby, we could see the *Aurania* anchored in the bay. From the shore she looked quite undamaged, but Jack told us there was a hole in her side big enough to drive a double-decker bus through. Obviously, she would be out of commission for a while.

We stayed at Helensburgh for only a short time and then, with Jack still on leave, set off for the south of England. My mother was then living in a small flat at the back of Cecil's office. He was now well established in England with his own firm of solicitors in Lymington High Street. My mother had stayed in Southampton through the worst of the Blitz. The house in Portland Terrace was in an extremely vulnerable position overlooking the Docks and Pirelli's factory, and bombs rained down on all sides. She was there through the worst of the air-raids and occupied her time helping at the air raid warden's canteen and making tea at her house for those on duty and thoroughly enjoyed the excitement of it all and making herself useful. It transformed her life and dulled the pain of losing my father and of our going abroad.

However Cecil decided it was far too dangerous for her to remain where she was and persuaded her to move to Lymington and comparative safety. I think she missed her old life and surroundings, but settled down to the more provincial existence of a country town, happy as long as some of the family, at least, were not far away. We stayed with her for a while but it was a tight squeeze in so small a flat, so I soon managed to find a house to rent at Brockenhurst, a few miles from Lymington. The house was very large and fortunately furnished, with a beautiful garden stocked full of flowers and vegetables. We were very lucky indeed to find such a place, but in wartime Britain, the population was comparatively small with many service personnel overseas, so accommodation was not at the premium it is now. There was usually little difficulty in finding a place to rent.

Just before we were due to move in, some of the radiators burst, flooding most of the ground floor and ruining a very valuable piano (not ours of course). While repairing the damage and drying the place out, the builders set fire to the great chimney in the 30 foot long sitting room. The fire service was called out and once more the poor old house was saturated with water. In time, things settled down and we moved in. Now, in place of Canadian woodlands, there was once again the beautiful New Forest to roam in, botany expeditions and places to explore. Shelagh, now seventeen and a half, had joined the WRNS. She had been drafted to Lowton St Mary in Lancashire to train as a wireless telegraphist and we would only see her when she came home on leave. Nice as it was, the house was now far too large. With the boys away at boarding school, Shelagh in the Wrens and Jack far away in Scotland, I was by myself most of the time, so at the end of the tenancy I rejoined Jack.

We found ourselves back in Glasgow staying at an hotel in Rutherglen. The hospitality there was not as we found at our first port of call. Courses served at mealtimes were so minute we felt forever famished. After a week's semi-starvation we moved on to another hotel on the other side of the city which was much more congenial.

On a visit to Edinburgh, I wandered into Jenners in Princes Street and discovering that the store included an estate agent, migrated towards it like a bee to a honey pot. I had discovered a new obsession, looking at houses for rent. Needless to say, there were many more available then than there are now. The young agent unhesitatingly recommended a property in a district known as Lochgelly. He said it had a view from the back over Loch Leven with the old castle on the shore and it was surrounded by lovely countryside. From the front he went on, waxing more and more lyrical, it looked over fields of narcissi to the distant horizon and the green hills beyond. It sounded almost too good to be true.

While I was dithering, the agent rang the owner, who urged me to meet her there that afternoon so I could see the property for myself. Lochgelly itself was a mining town, but the house was situated outside the main residential district in what was indeed beautiful countryside. I was so delighted with everything I saw that day that we moved in the next week. I arranged for John to attend the little Catholic school at Cowdenbeath and later, the Abbey School at Fort Augustus on Loch Ness. Francis was to go to the preparatory school at Carlekemp.

The house was a bit old-fashioned and a little shabby, like a favourite well-worn old coat, comfortable, warm and welcoming. The only means of heating the place appeared to be the high iron basket fireplaces, which were attractive, but they looked as if keeping warm might prove to be expensive. Nevertheless, we needed heat, so I duly ordered coal. The capacious cellar roof hinged back so that fuel could be emptied into it via the back garden. I was out shopping when the coalman called, but he had been there many times before he said, and knew exactly where it was to go. I expected the few sacks I had ordered to just about cover the cellar floor but on my return to my horror, I found the place filled to the roof with good quality coal which was even flowing onto the pathway. "This is going to cost a fortune!" I thought, hurrying to the telephone to ring the fuel merchants. When I got through, I was told that as coal was only twelve shillings and sixpence a ton, they thought I could do with a bit extra!

One of the bedroom doors had a Yale lock. I wondered about this and several theories presented themselves. Perhaps the former owners or tenants kept their valuables in there and it doubled as an extra-large safe. Or perhaps someone was overly modest and did not want their privacy intruded upon while undressing for bed. Or - more romantically - as in *Wuthering Heights*, a lunatic was kept there. The reality was different from all these speculations. At the post office where I enquired, I was told: "It was a hoose for inebriates and those suffering from DTs were always put in that room. Did ye no ken?"

Lochgelly was composed largely of little terraced houses, homes of the miners and their families. I went the rounds of some of them with a friend, collecting for a Church of Scotland charity, and was surprised at the contrast in the interiors. Through an open door, one could glimpse a spotlessly clean room with everything in its place, the table laid with a white cloth and sparkling dishes. Another might have grubby children crawling over a filthy floor, broken toys everywhere, and unwashed crockery littering the table and sink. It was quite often from the latter that my friend and I received the most generous response.

John, Francis and I (also Jack when he was home) attended the Catholic church in Lochgelly. The priest had barely time to leave the altar after the last blessing when there was a tremendous clattering of boots and heavy shoes over the tiled floor and in no time at all, the church which had been filled to capacity, was empty. Apparently everyone was anxious to get to the pub and be first in the queue. From the frequent sermons on the subject, I gathered a good deal of the weekly wage packet changed hands there, and wives and children consequently went short. Churches of all denominations strongly disapproved of this practice, but could do little to stop it.

Lochgelly also boasted at that time the only parliamentary candidate, a man called Gallagher.

After we had been at the house in Lochgelly for about five months, our tenancy period was coming to an end and as the owner wished now to live there herself, we had to be on the move again, this time rather regretfully. Francis and John were now both at Fort Augustus Abbey School as Carlekemp, the prep school for the Abbey, was now amalgamated with the main establishment for the remainder of the war.

At about this time, Jack received a new appointment. He was to be King's Harbour Master at Kyle of Lochalsh. During his intervening leave, we stayed for a short while at Dunfermline, intending to travel to Kyle together to find somewhere to live. Neither of us thought there would be any difficulty in my accompanying him, despite the district being in a prohibited area. To make sure and to avoid delays, we visited the head of the local police the day before our departure and received an assurance that as I was travelling with my husband, there should be no difficulty.

This proved to be somewhat optimistic. When we got to the station and gave the name of our destination to the army officer in charge, he stated emphatically that without certain papers and accredited references from magistrate or priest, I would not be allowed beyond the boundaries of the prohibited zone at Achnasheen. This was a bit of a blow. Until Jack's train was due to leave we discussed whether it might be better for me to remain in Dunfermline or proceed to Achnasheen. I decided it would be better to be halfway than have to remain behind.

We were told there was a small hotel in Achnasheen where I could stay, it was in fact the only building there, but I might have to wait some time for permission to proceed to Kyle. Feeling very deflated, we took our seats on the train and travelled almost in silence until we reached Achnasheen, me pondering the fact I must have appeared a very suspicious character to the army authorities! On arrival at Achnasheen I was rather unceremoniously escorted from the carriage by two soldiers, one on each side of me, and led to the little hotel. By now, I was beginning to feel like some dangerous criminal, but once at the hotel, they left me on my own.

As expected, the situation was beautiful, but as isolated

as anywhere could be. In peacetime, the little hotel was used as a fishing inn and I have never known as clean, bright and warm a hostelry in all our wanderings. What was more, the food was the best I have ever sampled. The price per week all-in was TWO POUNDS!

I was there for some weeks with very little company but in idyllic surroundings. What struck me most forcibly was that those living in and around the district needed to produce only one identification paper to pass freely from one zone to another as often as they pleased, whereas service personnel and their families had all this vetting to go through accompanied by stern warnings of careless talk etc. and were only allowed one exit permit per year. Yet the locals seemed to talk freely about anything and everything, including troop movements on their doorstep, without apparent let or hindrance. Not that there were many military secrets to talk about in sleepy little Achnasheen.

Since I did not fish or hunt deer, after about a month of kicking my heels, I began to feel a bit bored and was thankful when at last I was free to proceed to Kyle. Armed with about twenty different papers, I finally said goodbye to the hotel manager and his wife who had looked after me so well and the friendly guests (service personnel mostly) and set off for Kyle. It seemed an age since Jack and I were together and it was lovely to see him again.

"Where are we staying this time?" I asked, and was told "In someone's office." A local businessman had offered to let us have on a temporary basis a small building which had been originally intended as an office situated at the bottom of his garden. It consisted of two sitting rooms and a cubby-hole with washbasin and lavatory. Kyle was crowded out, Jack told me, and this was all he could find, and we were thankful for it. A Mrs Macrae kindly supplied us with a bed, some curtains, chairs, a table and rugs. I bought some cheap crockery, knives and forks etc. together with a couple of cooking utensils. The place by now, was beginning to look almost cosy.

Every other family in Kyle seemed to have the surname Macrae, including the butcher, baker and milkman, yet none claimed relationship to any of the others. The milkman at first declared he had not sufficient milk to supply us, a statement I knew to be untrue. But we were foreigners and had to wait to be accepted into the community. I bought a tin of condensed milk on points until the situation was sorted out.

That evening, waiting in a queue with Jack outside the camp cinema, someone tapped me on the shoulder. "Mistress Locke" said a quiet voice. "If ye come round to the shop in the morning, I'll gie ye a pint of milk." We were still comparative strangers of course, but our presence in Kyle had been approved and accepted and we able from then to obtain supplies of milk.

There was a certain air of anarchy among the Kyle shopkeepers. Rationing was most unpopular with them and they hated the constantly changing prices. I suspect also that they resented being told what to do by rules emanating from far-off Whitehall. Since far larger amounts of consumer goods had been allocated to the area because of the floating service population, rather than let anything perish, they were quite prepared to sell surpluses with or without points if the purchasers were known to them and could be trusted. Consequently, scarcities of any commodity were almost unknown and rationing practically non-existent. No one complained.

It was essential to find larger accommodation before the school holidays and Shelagh's leave. In desperation we finally located a top floor flat owned by a well-known fisherman and his daughter, the latter studying at Aberdeen University. They would only rent us the flat on condition we agreed to look after her ageing father, cook his meals, make his bed etc. Since by that time we were getting pretty desperate, we agreed.

While staying there I acquired a second cat. The first had been Scrabstitch, a tabby who was fed daily in the Mess and who decided to adopt us. Then Jack brought home a tiny kitten that had lost its mother in an accident.

Scrabstitch had a friend, a poor half-starved multi-coloured stray with whom he had great games in the garden belonging to the house. The 'friend' took the kitten under its wing (as it were), licking it and fondling it. The poor thing seemed to be asking for a home too (as a babysitter). We could not refuse and found ourselves in possession of a third cat. But after returning from a short leave in the south of England, on our return, we discovered the poor kindly stray had starved to death in the garden. We had arranged with the daughter of the house to feed the cats while we were away, which she promised to do, and we left them plenty of food, but this one she had ignored. We were most upset. It had been a lovely cat, friendly and affectionate and had asked for so little. While we were away, it had been deliberately shut out and left to fend for itself. We were therefore not sorry to move from these digs into the Kyle of Lochalsh Hotel when we were given rooms there.

We now had a lovely room overlooking the Sound, a dream of a bed and large private bathroom with lashings of hot water. The food was absolutely wonderful and because we were counted as service personnel, we paid less than half hotel charges. They agreed to accommodate the children there too when they were home.

The winter we spent in that part of Scotland was wet and warm and we made one visit to Skye. We took Shelagh over there to see the misty Cuillins at closer quarters and to organise an expedition to Loch Coruisk. There was only one local hotel, run by a jovial character called Jimmy Campbell, who was glad to see some fresh faces and was lavish with his invitations to free drinks. We were his only out-of-season visitors, yet in spite of this, every table in the dining room was beautifully laid, with immaculate white cloths and vases of fresh flowers.

Unfortunately for the proposed expedition, a thick mist suddenly descended as the ferry landed us at the quay. It came down to about a foot off the ground and our exploration of the Loch had to be cancelled. We dared not even leave the hotel for fear of getting hopelessly lost in that vast lonely landscape. The mist did not clear during the three days we were on the Island, but as we boarded the ferry for the return journey, just as suddenly as it had descended, the fog lifted and soon the mountains were again revealed in the fitful sunshine. Was Skye trying to tell us Sassenachs something or having a joke at our expense?

We had been in Kyle a year when Jack received another posting, this time to Glasgow. Finding a new home in that district was not difficult as a kind friend stepped into the breach and offered us her small house in Chryston on the Stirling Road at the foot of the Campsie Hills. Glen Cottage, as it was called, was an attractive little place set in a large rough garden with a stream running through it and a mass of beautiful rhododendrons at the back of the house.

Once again, we acquired pets (we always found good homes for those we left behind). This time, I got myself a young Alsatian for protection, as in Scotland there were no trespassing laws at the time and anyone who happened to fancy it could and did walk over the garden and round the house, day or night. We named the dog Micky. As he grew older he rather overdid his guard dog duties by biting the postman and knocking out two of his teeth. Also, he would allow no one, friend or foe, near the house. Inconvenient, to say the least. So Mick had to be found a home where his watchdog talents would not be wasted on innocent visitors like our poor postman.

I advertised in the *Glasgow Daily Herald*. The afternoon the ad appeared, thirty people came to offer themselves as new owners. I did not clinch the deal there and then, and perhaps it was just as well, for Micky's guardian angel was hovering overhead. In the evening, well after dark, a young couple rang the bell and surprisingly, for once, Micky did not even bark. What was even more surprising, after they had entered and were sitting down, he strolled in, laid his head on the young man's feet and quietly went to sleep. We assumed that by this action, he had made his own choice. Collar and lead were fetched and he went off with his new owners seemingly perfectly happy and without a backward glance. Having met that young couple I felt that he had found a good and happy home. His behaviour had been impeccable and looked as if it might remain so. I never heard otherwise, so perhaps he turned into an older and wiser dog.

Cecil came to visit us at Glen Cottage with his second wife Cecilia. They were our first staying visitors and must have found the quietness of the Scottish countryside a great relief after the bombing of London where they were then living. On his departure, Cecil said he would help with the boys' school fees and we gladly accepted his kind offer. He was then a Squadron Leader in the RAF based at Bush House, his solicitor's business carried on in his absence by reliable and competent staff. I think they enjoyed their visit, and we certainly did. Situated as we were miles away from the bombing in England, we hardly knew there was a war on, and with no petrol for anyone and therefore no private motor cars, the countryside was incredibly peaceful.

While in Glasgow, we paid one or two visits to the boys' school at Fort Augustus. The Abbey was based at a lovely spot not far from Fort William and the towering heights of Ben Nevis. The boys took us for walks up the rugged valley of the Tarf and over to the opposite side of the Loch, where a large white house belonging to the Hambro family dominated the scene. At that time, the Benedictine monks supplied the whole of the village with electricity generated from a stream flowing down a hillside in the grounds. Many a fine salmon graced their table from the loch, and besides growing their own vegetables, they kept bees. The skeps were situated some way from the abbey itself in the garden of a haunted house called Adachy Lodge. The former owner, then deceased, had apparently practised the Black Mass or some such satanic rite and fearful happenings were supposed to have ensued. The monks once tried to let the house as a boarding establishment, but after one night, no visitor would remain under its roof any longer. The locals avoided the place like the plague and nothing would induce any of them to even enter its front door. When we saw it, it was already falling into complete decay, the roof fallen in and the interior a shambles. I wonder what it looks like now? That is, if it still exists.

One night on the 9th of May, 1945, we heard the wonderful sound of church bells heralding the end of the war in Europe. Although it was one of the least of our wartime worries, the blackout had been such a blight on our lives that it was no wonder people went mad on the streets of Glasgow and other cities throughout the country. At last, a new beginning for us all, or so we hoped at the time. My mother-in-law had died while we were away in Canada and Jack's brother and his wife Lorna were looking after my father-in-law in his Southampton house. The latter had been a schoolteacher at four Southampton board schools from the beginning of the century until about

1929. The pupils came from very poor families and disease and malnourishment among them was rife. There were occasional outings and a rally on Empire Day at which Father-in-law would deliver a stirring oration on the greatness of the British Empire, exhorting his young audience to become worthy citizens by always "playing the game", after which there would be a rendering of *Land of Hope and Glory*. He was a very patriotic man.

Uncle James and hard Aunt Elsie had also died and 'poor Hilda' had at last managed to break free from her bonds and taken herself off to live in Leckhampton, near Cheltenham, in a flat she shared with Flossie for a while after the latter had become widowed. "Aunt Puss" and Uncle Ben had also died and my cousin Desmond had come out of the Home Guard to resume his legal profession. Most of my father's relations were no longer in the land of the living, but my mother's sisters were all still intact and scattered round the world in one foreign country or another.

We now received a letter from our landlords, the owners of Glen Cottage, to say that they were now back from abroad and would like to take over the house again, giving us due notice to quit. At about the same time we also learned that before returning to his old company, the Cunard White Star Line, Jack was scheduled to go to Egypt for a year or so in his capacity as an officer in the Royal

Naval Reserve. We were of course still at war with Japan and he was not yet due for demob. He remained for the time being in Glasgow until early in 1947, when he had two weeks' leave prior to leaving for the Middle East.

On a warm spring afternoon, we said goodbye once more and he travelled to London to join his ship. We planned to meet up again soon when I had obtained the necessary visas and had the statutory inoculations. His letters home told of the hot sunshine and deep blue of the sea and of the luxury of life in Egypt, which I hoped I would soon be able to share. It all sounded such a contrast to the Scottish mists and rain. Meanwhile, in cold, sober England, I was beginning to despair of ever being able join him. I was having a terrible time convincing the Egyptian authorities that I had a genuine reason for wanting to visit their country and was neither a saboteur nor a spy. The injections had long been finished with, yet over and over again I had to make these fruitless calls on the Egyptian Embassy in London. Altogether, I made fifteen visits there and even in the days of cheap rail travel, this involved considerable expense.

Jack and I had seen more of each other during wartime than in all our previous married years. The Navy had been far more generous with leave than Cunard and now I was beginning to feel lost and lonely without him. I suppose I had become dependent on his company and support and the frustrating three months without him were beginning to get me down. It was difficult to sleep at night and a sense of depression developed and almost threatened to overwhelm me at times. We had both looked forward to my being in Egypt long before this. I found myself beginning to lose interest in any social life at home and with all the disappointments and worry about Jack himself, I came almost to the brink of despair.

He had never been a sociable person. The numerous parties, cocktail gatherings and other entertainment laid on for the British contingent frankly bored him. Since attendance at some of these gatherings was almost compulsory, he hated the small talk and with me by his side, might have enjoyed it, since he could take more of a back seat. Always a heavy smoker, he had increased his intake and had developed a slight cough which was, he wrote, especially noticeable in the mornings or when the weather was exceptionally dry. No one then was aware just how bad smoking was for the health.

Chapter Eleven

Egypt

On what was to be my last visit to the Embassy, when I had finally almost given up hope, I heard to my immense relief that the visa had been granted and I was free to arrange my passage. I set sail a week or two later on one of the newer of the Union Castle liners and with our reunion at the other end to look forward to, should have enjoyed the voyage. But once again, I was laid low with seasickness which showed no sign of abating throughout the journey.

As the ship neared the Egyptian coastline with the intense heat beating down on the decks, I joined the other passengers on the top deck to be interviewed by customs officers, feeling like a limp dishrag. Jack came out on the tender to meet me and ran up the gangway. I was waiting at the top like a pale wan shadow and his arms went round me in a bear-like hug. It was a superb moment to see him again, deeply sun-tanned and as handsome as ever. Suddenly, I felt on top of the world. We kissed again and again and were both so happy, the loneliness of the past months forgotten.

Jack had booked a room for us at Caffe's Pension, a guest house run by a Greek woman. It was an excellent choice, spacious, bright and comparatively cheap and with a lovely view over the tops of palm trees to a deep blue sparkling sea. Everything seemed set fair. But the following day, before I could begin to enjoy life again, a devastating attack of 'gippy tummy' descended and for the next two days, I could neither eat nor move from my bed. It was an unfortunate introduction to Egypt.

Once fully recovered, I spent the mornings exploring Port Said, shopping or watching the cosmopolitan crowds milling around and along the main street, or going in and out of the small restaurants, of which there were many. Everywhere the white houses gleamed in the shimmering light, the pink and purple bougainvillea flowed down walls in a tide of colour and nearby, in the Garden of the Monks attached to the Catholic Church, the jacaranda trees with their clusters of mauve bell-like flowers drooped above the green grass. And over all this splendour, the scorching sun shone from a brilliant blue sky.

Sometimes we would walk along the banks of the Suez Canal watching the ships, big and small, slowly steaming their way to Aden. So near were they that it seemed one had only to stretch out a hand to touch them. Giant lanterns were fixed to the bows of each vessel. As we walked on and left the town, to the right of us shimmered the Great Salt Lake and on the left bank, further on where a waterway joined the canal itself, a sign announced, "Palestine". Everything everywhere was dead flat, the horizon viewed from any direction unbroken by landmarks. It was a strange, almost eerie landscape.

It was not long before I was drawn into Port Said society. When it became known that I played bridge, Englishwomen popped up all over the place with invitations to games that seemed to go on all day, accompanied by numerous gins and whiskies. "Such clean drinks" one addicted lady remarked. The puritanical side of my conscience was at first horrified to be asked to morning bridge parties, but I stopped feeling guilty when I realised there was really not much else for women with few interests, to do out here. So-called 'boys' did all the housework and cooking and were far better at food shopping than we could have been. Many of the shops were owned by the houseboy's friends, from whom they invariably got a discount not passed onto the employer, and who can blame them?

Halfway through Jack's assignment, he was drafted to Alexandria and although we later went back to Caffe's, for the time being we moved into a hotel there. I was anxious to see the city and it was a relief to get away from bridge for a while. Alexandria was by no means a friendly place for the British just then, but Port Said was no better in that respect. Riots had taken place in both districts for some time past against the English presence and while we were at Caffe's, at least one noisy crowd had bashed its way through the town, hurling bricks at windows, hitting people with sticks and stones and breaking the head off Boadicea's statue on the Front.

Hatred of the British was even more evident in Alex. We heard that a short while before our arrival, a British sailor had been decapitated and his head carried round the city on the end of a knife, although I cannot vouch for the truth of this story. Cruelty to animals was rife. Poor half-starved mules would be driven along the streets, their sides sore and bleeding from the rough and heavy loads they carried, and if it was thought their pace was too slow, they were whipped unmercifully. I once saw a boy deliberately break a puppy's leg, but dared not remonstrate. If I had, in seconds a menacing crowd would collect and I would be lucky to get out of the situation unhurt. I found this aspect of Egypt depressing. It was a dark element in an otherwise interesting and beautiful land. In my mind, I somehow linked it with the absence of twilight in that strange country. One moment, the sun would be shining brightly from a clear blue sky. Within minutes, a glowing red orb would be disappearing below the horizon leaving land and sea in darkness.

The shopping centre of Alexandria boasted some fine French couturier establishments, much too expensive for me but I liked to look in the windows, pretend I was terribly rich and array myself mentally in some of their gorgeous garments. When I did buy an article in a more modest emporium, it was disconcerting to ask for it in what I thought was perfectly correct French and be answered in excellent English - and I thought I had a good accent!

At our hotel I met a prim, well-dressed elderly little lady. We became quite friendly and one day she asked me if I would care to meet her for morning coffee in one of Alex's smarter cafes. Since she dressed and behaved very much like Queen Victoria and appeared most aristocratic, it was more like a royal command, and I was quite flattered by the invitation. We agreed to meet at Baudrot's the following day. The weather that morning was cooler, so we were able to sit out on the pleasant balcony. Coffee was brought and we prepared to exchange a bit of gossip and cheerful conversation. But before either of us had a chance to say a word, the window of an upstairs flat just above us suddenly opened, and in the middle of the table between our two cups landed, of all objects, a used sanitary towel. Someone in that flat had evidently heard the sound of two English voices when we ordered the coffee and decided to show us what they thought of us. It could not have been a more potent insult. My friend's normally dignified and regal features turned purple with rage and disgust. But what made matters far worse was the Arab waiter, who gingerly picked up the article between finger and thumb, placed it on a large silver tray and addressing my poor mortified friend said loudly "Is this yours, Madam?" She flashed him a truly murderous look, got up hastily and rushed out, leaving me to pay the bill. I could hardly blame her, for so calculated an insult piled on insult was quite outrageous. I was feeling pretty shaken myself, but not wanting to draw out the incident any more than necessary, meekly left some money and made my own exit. I wondered later whether she had complained to the management. Perhaps we both should have. When I returned to the hotel she had checked out and I saw her no more.

When we had been in Alex for about a month, a friend who was about to return home on a long leave lent us his comfortable flat on the Rue Fouad overlooking the Sporting Club at the front and the Smouha Racing Ground at the back, both scenes of exciting equestrian events. From the first floor balcony I had a good view of all the races and was often astonished at some of the dirty tactics of the Arab jockeys. If they were in the lead towards the end of a race and in danger of being overtaken by a following horse, these fellows would use the whip, not on their own mounts, but they would turn right round in the saddle and hit the challenging animal on the nose!

With our flat went a 'boy' of about fifty years. He was a wonderful cook, whether company was expected or not, but housework, which was also part of his duties, he was averse to. Dust was thick everywhere, but it was not considered correct for me to openly remedy this state of affairs, so when he was out shopping, I took advantage of his absence to surreptitiously clean out the whole place thoroughly. Whether or not he ever noticed the transformation on his return was not apparent. He never mentioned it, and neither of course did I.

Jack and I attended the Italian Cathedral for Mass one Sunday morning and were somewhat distracted from the impassioned sermon preached in Italian by the fiery little priest by a large bug which was slowly but determinedly making its way up the back of the person in front. On going to Confession in the same church and being bitten by dozens of these insects crawling up our legs, we made a hurried exit, unconfessed.

We decided we could not possibly leave Egypt without seeing Cairo. It was a scorchingly hot day, although less humid than of late, when we boarded the little train. A sandstorm blew up during the journey, much of the fine sand percolating under the carriage window-frame and settling on our clothes, up our noses and into our eyes and mouths. In less than half an hour, the storm subsided, leaving our carriage an inch deep in sand. The train stopped for a while at Ismalia, where the flame trees were a picture. They seemed to grow everywhere, the brilliant red flowers shimmering in the bright sunshine. I once sent, quite illegally, a pod home to my sister-in-law, who was a knowledgeable gardener, hoping it might germinate in her greenhouse, but in spite of every care, nothing happened. The pod eventually dried up and had to be burnt.

Our first impression on arrival in Cairo was one of prevailing shabbiness and neglect, but one could say that of many English towns in the vicinity of railway stations. Shepheards Hotel had recently been burnt down and several districts were unsafe for Europeans, so we made Giza our destination and that held us spellbound. Looking across the sandy desert to the far horizon, a strange feeling of tranquillity gradually enveloped the senses. It was a most soporific landscape. An ancient Arab told our fortunes in the sand, poking it into shapes and murmuring incantations. Only one person was allowed with him at a time, the others present being requested to remain out of earshot. Judging by this demand, we were fairly sure he told everyone the same thing!

The rest of the day was spent in the famous Cairo Museum, which lived up to its reputation in every respect. Would-be guides pestered us on all sides, so the first thing to do was to find an honest-looking one and stick to him. We were lucky in our choice and once fixed up, the rest gave us no further trouble.

The ancient Egyptians must have been a handsome lot, to judge by the faces on the many statues in the museum, including of course that of Tutankhamun. There was so much to see and it was getting late. We could have spent many hours longer in that fascinating place and listening to the stories portrayed by the hieroglyphics around the walls, but our guide's time was up. So fascinating had the visit been that we had missed lunch, and regretfully had to leave.

While enjoying a belated tea on the balcony of a hotel overlooking the Nile and gazing into its murky depths, I marvelled at the legend that those who drink it always return. On the contrary, it seemed to me that they would not live long enough to return. We stayed a week in Cairo exploring its many attractions and did not risk drinking the Nile water but bade farewell to this marvellous city with the wish that we might come back again despite this omission. I suspect the legend of drinking the Nile water is a bit like the one about kissing the Blarney Stone. With the one, you risk imbibing fatal streptococci, with the other, you are in grave danger of breaking your neck.

For Jack of course, duty called and so it was back, firstly to Alex, then to Port Said again, where our last domicile was a guest house with the almost Hollywood-sounding name of 'House of the Palms'. It seemed that we might at any moment come across Peter Lorre, Charles Boyer or Peter Ustinov in one or other of their film roles. Needless to say, none made their appearance but from our bedroom window, we did have a marvellous view of the De Lesseps statue at the end of the quay and could look across the sea with the sure knowledge that we would soon be on our way home again.

We left for home in early September and were seen off by our good friends, a Naval Paymaster and his wife armed with flowers and fruit for the voyage on the *Caernavon Castle*. Glorious weather and calm seas prevailed during the first part of the journey and the route took us round the Greek Islands, which were still mined from the recent war, so lifejackets had to be kept at the ready and only a narrow seaway had to be kept as far as Greece. I would have loved to have gone ashore at Athens and Jack shared my wish, but for security reasons it was not allowed, the authorities fearing that undesirable stowaways or arms might be smuggled in among the passengers. So we could only stand at the rails and gaze across at the Acropolis rising in the distance.

Sunshine and calm seas continued until we reached Malta, but once anchored in the Grand Harbour, I noticed with trepidation the increasing wind and rising waves. I must confess I have almost a phobia about seasickness, but as it happened, all was well. The ship docked at Southampton after a pleasant voyage and we were met there by my mother and Francis. It was lovely to see them again, looking brown and fit after what had been a beautiful English summer and to acclimatise us, the weather very kindly stayed that way well into the autumn.

My mother had rented a pretty cottage in the High Street, Lymington, and we stayed with her, since Jack still had a few weeks' leave due to him after concluding his foreign service. When this was up he rejoined his old company, Cunard, and took command of a passenger-cum-cargo ship sailing from London. Once more, there was the question of finding somewhere to live. I wrote and telephoned various agents all over the south of England and in due course heard of a likely property to be let furnished on a short lease. It was described as a charming property of great character, as well as being spacious and comfortable. It was called 'The Old Mill' and was at Sheet, near Petersfield.

Chapter Twelve

On the move again – and again

The River Rother ran alongside the garden and a tributary of it flowed under the house itself. It was overlooked at the back by a wooden platform, from which we managed to catch quite a few delicious trout, enjoyed fresh for breakfast. There was a frequent train service from Petersfield to Waterloo, so Jack was able come down for all but the shortest leaves. John, now in the Navy as an instructor, also came down often to visit us. That winter the house was inclined to be damp and cold, as charming houses of character often are. Since the stream ran through the cellar and when in spate, rose alarmingly to a few feet of the kitchen floor, I had visions of a Noah's Ark situation, but it never went beyond that stage, I am glad to say.

Petersfield had a weekly market and cycling into town for shopping, I noticed the auctioneer still asking for bids for what looked like a cardboard box with holes punched in it, although the sales were over. He was banging the box up and down on the counter and I asked him what was inside. "Day-old ducklings" was the reply. I felt so sorry for the poor little fellows that I bought them. Fitting the box carefully into the bicycle basket, I was about to leave when I was called back and told that I had bought not one, but three boxes of ducklings, nine birds in all.

Having set out with the intention of purchasing the usual household commodities and returning with the foundation of a farmyard, I now had to consider the welfare of the new charges. I raised them in a wooden case beside the kitchen stove and when they were big enough, I taught them to swim in a small pool beside the river. Not surprisingly, they were quick learners.

When the lease on the Old Mill was up and we would soon have to be on our way again, our nine ducks presented a problem. They still looked on the kitchen as their proper home and me as the mother duck, and they would all troop in at mealtimes with a great deal of quacking and glad flapping of wings. But as luck would have it, on our departure some kind neighbours who owned a large pond offered to take them and promised they would be kept as pets only. We knew they would keep their promise as they were good friends of ours and as they would be well supplied with eggs, the new menagerie would not be entirely unproductive.

Our new rented house was on the busy main road that led from Lymington to Brockenhurst and just before settling in, we found ourselves the owners of a Blue Persian cat. My mother had bought it on the spur of the moment, but she was away a lot and could find no one to take over in her absence. She was a lovely little cat called 'Boo' - no idea why.

Boo was accident-prone. Not long after we had her, her tail was bitten off by a fox. The vet could do nothing to save the tail and Boo ended up looking more like a Manx than a Persian.

Just across the road was an enticing-looking coppice. Although our house had a fairly ample garden, Boo had decided to explore further. A dustcart was moving slowly up the road and a car, driven very fast, overtook it, ran over Boo and disappeared out of sight in a blue haze. The driver of the dustcart tenderly picked up the poor lifeless body, carried her into the garden and gave her to me. I was grateful someone with a kind heart had been on hand. Poor Boo. She was so gentle and friendly and I had become very fond of her.

We did not stay long in Lymington. The owner of the house wanted to sell, so we moved to Sussex. This time, we bought. The house had been up for auction and did not reach the reserve price. Cecil negotiated a mortgage and we obtained it comparatively cheaply. We managed to collect various bits of furniture at sales in the neighbourhood and soon had enough to enable us to move in and make the little house habitable and attractive. It had no electricity, but was completely wired for it and with pylons ready to connect, the auctioneer assured us the service would be connected within a very short time. The house included a large meadow and prolific vegetable garden. It had been built on the site of a much older dwelling.

That summer the branches of the plum trees broke under their load. There were William pears galore and on one old lichened tree were the juiciest, sweetest apples I have ever tasted. We picked fifteen pounds of blackcurrants as large as grapes in one afternoon. Peas and beans flourished like weeds. All this cornucopia had been there for years, never planted by us.

The electricity never came. That vital adjunct to modern living and the lack of it taught us how dependent upon it we had become. Candles fell over and dropped grease everywhere. Paraffin lamps either flared up, scorching the nearby wall and cracking the glass glove, or went out. Soot floated all over the house and settled on carpets and furniture. The first night we spent there, two water pipes under the bathroom basin burst, so the local plumber had to be called out at 10 pm. to prevent the upstairs been completely flooded. He attributed this catastrophe to very high water pressure owing to the slope on which the house was built, but we soon discovered it was bad workmanship done on a shoestring. To our cost, we had stupidly decided to dispense with the services of a surveyor, which proved to be false economy, and we had only ourselves to blame.

After we had moved in, we heard a local rumour that at one time, John Haigh, known as the 'Acid Bath Murderer', had once lived there. It seemed quite feasible as the site was very isolated. If ever a house was haunted by mishap, this one was. Dry-rot manifested itself beside the fireplace and in the roof joists. The staircase led directly up from the sitting room and in spite of heavy curtains, there was no way we could keep out the draughts. Yet the little house in its Sussex countryside, surrounded by fields sloping down to an enchanting brook, looked beautiful.

A woman came to see me one day and said that if ever I wanted to sell, she was willing to buy the place, as she wanted to put caravans on the site. I seriously considered this suggestion. We eventually agreed to her offer and were once more on the move. We had selected a house in Uckfield for our next residence and this time, employed a surveyor who gave it the thumbs down. It was winter and

I caught the flu. My mother came down to nurse me through it and when I recovered, I accompanied her back to Lymington.

The next definite port of call was a house lent by a friend who was going to Australia to visit relatives. Again, it was in the heart of the New Forest near Brockenhurst, no near neighbours and surrounded on all sides by forest land. I felt a little nervous there all on my own and one night called the police because I thought I saw two escaped prisoners-of-war in the garden. There was a camp nearby with as yet unrepatriated POWs still in residence. The two 'escapees' turned out to be a couple of donkeys which had managed to break their way through the garden hedge and were peacefully grazing on the lawn.

In the late spring, my brother Mervyn, his wife and baby daughter came to stay. There is no better time in the Forest. The gorze blazed a trail everywhere, the surrounding woods were full of primroses and bluebells, and newborn foals chased each other and gambolled around their unconcerned grazing mothers. It was then early 1950. We went for long walks and picnicked and in the still dark evenings, we sat around the fire discussing the day's events, listening to music on the wireless or simply reading or dozing. Mervyn had a small Morris Minor and took me on a tour of estate agents' windows. Yes, we were still looking for somewhere permanent to live!

Driving slowly up the narrow congested Highcliffe High Street, I caught a fleeting glimpse of the photograph of a white cottage in one of them. At my urgent request, Mervyn parked, and I jumped out of the car, ran back and digested the particulars. It was pouring with rain, but when I returned, already dripping wet from this brief excursion, I begged him to take me to the site of this cottage "just to have a look at the outside". It was a Saturday and the agency was closed, so it was not possible to obtain an order to view.

'Mill Cottage', judging by its picture, had a most charming appearance. It seemed just the right size for us and I knew Burley to be an attractive village. We overshot the mark on the first attempt at finding it and then got bogged down in thick mud and fallen leaves trying to turn the car around. Curtains of heavy rain were still falling as we peered as closely as possible through the misted windows, but the photograph in the agent's windows had not lied. It looked in reality just as portrayed, and I decided then and there, that this was to be our next house.

During most of this time, Jack was at sea. As in pre-war days, I saw him only infrequently. To the children when they were growing up, he was almost a stranger. A career in the merchant service is not conducive to close family life, and he must often have wondered where his next leave was to be spent. We seemed to be in a different place every time he came home, but I believe he enjoyed the constant changes of scenery as much as I did, although the continual moving house proved an awful drain on resources. We spent as we went and savings, it must be admitted, were almost nil. Long-suffering Cecil was as usual, brought into the business of obtaining a mortgage, arranging a survey and conducting the purchase of the property. Both Jack and I were hopeless at anything approaching legal transactions, although given a chance and the time to do it, Jack might well have managed perfectly well. But since he was generally somewhere in the vicinity of the Statue of Liberty at the crucial time and I had not a clue as to how to go about things, Cecil always came to the rescue. He never once criticised our chaotic way of living but merely concerned himself with a little gentle advice from time to time and was always ready with a helping hand free of charge. He must have been hard put to it sometimes not to say "for heaven's sake settle down in one place for more than six months at a time", but never did, and continued to be the kind, gentle, good-tempered baby brother I had always known and once been so jealous of. He was now well into his fifties and a discreet and dependable lawyer, not given to slapping people on the wrist, even his own sister. It might have been better for us if he had.

Incredibly, Mill Cottage became our home for six whole years! We did not attend Mass on Sundays now. The nearest church was in Ringwood and without a car, it was impossible to reach and we could find no one to give us a lift. Anyway, there weren't many Catholics in Burley. Not so bridge players. Word went round, and before long I was included in that charmed circle. The population of Burley, generally speaking, being on the rich side of affluent, we were invited to various cocktail parties. This was no new experience to Jack, who had been, and was at the time, Staff Captain on both the *Queen Mary* and *Queen Elizabeth*. He introduced a new cocktail to Burley society, not based on Vermouth and ice but a hot one, particularly welcome during the cold winter months. Unfortunately, I have forgotten the recipe. Around that time, we had plenty to celebrate. We had become grandparents for the first time, with the birth of a son to my eldest son John – christened inevitably John.

In that beautiful but isolated spot, transport was urgently needed. My father-in-law had recently died, leaving us a little money. We invested in a second-hand Morris Minor. Neither of us could drive, so being the one with more time to spare, I took lessons in Bournemouth, passed the test first time and drove home feeling very jubilant. Now we were mobile.

One worry loomed on the horizon. Jack was still smoking heavily, sometimes thirty a day. That winter he had suffered several mild attacks of bronchitis. He seemed otherwise fairly well, but nevertheless I felt a nagging unease about his health. The day before he was due back on the ship after an unusually prolonged leave, he complained of a pain in the calf of his left leg. There appeared no noticeable swelling, but a red line was faintly visible running up towards the knee. Around that line the pain was worse.

Our local doctor diagnosed phlebitis, but appeared not unduly perturbed. We did not altogether share his sanguine prognosis. "Should I remain home, do you think?" asked Jack. "I shall be on my feet all night getting the ship into Cherbourg." The doctor replied that he foresaw no danger of the clot travelling higher if care was taken not to knock the leg. So Jack, ever conscientious, left early the following morning to rejoin his ship.

That evening I received a phone call from him to say that the leg was a good deal worse and the ship's doctor would not take the responsibility of allowing him to proceed on the journey, considering there was a serious danger of pulmonary thrombosis. He was therefore being sent home on the Le Havre ferry. He arrived the next morning by taxi, looking pale, tired and obviously in pain.

Looking back on things today, I am surprised he was not sent straight to hospital, but evidently the medical authorities assumed he would be perfectly all right at home under surveillance of his own doctor and with me to look after him. At 10 pm the pain was much worse, having reached the groin. I rang the doctor. He was at a party and not pleased to be called but asked me which side was most painful. I answered "left". He said "OK, I'll be over first thing in the morning. Meanwhile, give him a couple of codeine tablets."

Jack, who had overheard the conversation from the bedroom, was none too pleased with me either. "The pain is on the right side, not the left" he grumbled. "Tried to make you hear me." Panic! "Acute appendicitis" I thought, and felt I had no option but to ring the doctor again. "I'll come over at once" he said tersely. He gave Jack some antibiotic pills, instructions to me on how to make him more comfortable and promised to be back first thing in the morning unless there were further developments.

I stayed up all night worrying, while Jack dozed now and then. When the doctor came in the morning, he took Jack's hand in both of his and shook it firmly, as if he was thankful to find him still alive. He did not suggest sending him to hospital, but simply recommended plenty of rest.

After a bad week Jack started to recover. We had a boxer dog called Toby who was a great comfort during hi convalescence. When Jack was better, he would take Toby for walks over the wild tract of forest at the end of our road. They would follow the stream across the grassland until it vanished into the woods leading to the outskirts of

Lyndhurst at Queen's Bower. Home again, Jack would relax in the armchair and Toby would lay a big floppy head on his slipper-clad feet and they would both fall peacefully asleep.

We lost Toby that summer. Usually full of beans, he grew lethargic and slow and a strange weakness developed in his forelegs. Jack, desperately worried, took him to vet after vet, but nothing could be done. Gradually Toby's whole body became completely paralysed until he could not even lift his head from the floor. He was only four years old when we had him put to sleep, and Jack was heartbroken. Man and dog had been inseparable. He had really loved that dog, we both had, and he had been a wonderful companion. He was very sadly missed.

Not long after, a letter arrived from the Cunard Company informing Jack he was to be placed on the retired list with six months' salary and a pension, the latter unfortunately much lower than if he had continued until official retirement age. He was then just over sixty.

Then my mother became ill. The trouble turned out to be appendicitis and when she left hospital, she went to a little nursing home to convalesce. Visiting her there, I was horrified to see how ill she looked and to hear from her own lips how ill she felt. The sister kept telling her that her age was against her, which did not help matters. She had always prided herself on being active for her age and looking younger than her years, and constant reference to anno domini had the effect of making her feel and look old for the first time in her life.

She eventually recovered, and resumed her old ways of getting up at the crack of dawn and boasting that she could get shopping and housework done efficiently by about nine-thirty, after which she could concentrate on her main interest, her little garden. But her recovery was short-lived. She died from a stroke a few months later.

She was the kindest person I have ever known and would give anyone her last penny, and frequently did. She was not well off. The solicitor's business in Southampton was sold after my father's death and the resulting income was just enough to see her through and pay for necessary expenditure. I am afraid Jack and I and the children took more advantage of her good nature and unfailing hospitality than perhaps we should have. She never refused any of us anything that was in her power to give, and this extended to close friends too. With her, we knew there was always a bed for the night, a hot meal on the table and sympathy always on hand when needed. The family meant everything to her. Although she might chide us gently sometimes, I never knew her to criticise any of us, even when we deserved it. She was a wonderful person. Her loss was hard to take.

Jack was now retired and had plenty of time on his

hands, but our expenses were mounting. Keeping up with the Joneses, or in our case, the cocktail and bridge circuit, was proving beyond our means, so we decided to look for greener grass elsewhere. We sold Mill Cottage for less than we had paid for it, a mad act we afterwards regretted, and rented a small property in Bolney, near Haywards Heath in Sussex, The house was some way from the shops and few buses passed the end of the road to Haywards or Crawley, the two nearest towns, so the Morris had to be kept for the time being. We were back on the old treadmill of having to travel miles for our shopping.

Shelagh came to stay with us that Christmas. I thought she looked thin in the face and tired, but assumed it must be due to the daily scrimmage of getting to work by tube every morning. She was working as a secretary in London. I was quite unprepared for the startling news she imparted to me one morning just before we were all due to go into Brighton for some Christmas shopping. She was kneeling on the hearthrug, her cold hands held out to the warmth of the fire, when she suddenly said without preamble "Mummy, I'm going to have a baby".

The words were said firmly and clearly, her eyes on my face to see how I would take the news. My heart leapt almost in fear not for myself, but for the repercussions I could foresee only too well. To a family like ours, her announcement was a tremendous blow. The so-called 'permissive society' was still a thing of the future and even today, my views on such a happening remain consistent. But when all was said and done, she was still my daughter and in spite of this shocking revelation, I intended to stand by her.

I have never seen my husband so angry. What he said was unrepeatable. The way he took the news made the whole affair assume a sordid aspect. His views on sex outside marriage were adamant, and had remained so throughout his life. At that moment, I think he considered our daughter had singlehandedly invented the permissive society and was the original Eve responsible for all the world's ills.

She had been going out for past twelve years with an Irishman who was more than twenty years older than herself. Long before they had met and when he was still very young, he had married a girl who, three days after their marriage, had run off with another man. He had only disclosed the fact that he was already married after Shelagh had known him for about ten years. She was then still a good Catholic and persuaded him to apply to the Church for an annulment on the grounds that his marriage had never been consummated. The Catholic Church, however, refused to believe this and the application failed.

For the remainder of that afternoon and evening, cold and desperate, Jack and I walked together up and down the lane arguing and arguing. I begged for tolerance, stressed the danger to our marriage because of his implacable views, begged for some measure of understanding, but all in vain. He would not unbend in the slightest degree, so eventually, cold and miserable, we retired to bed.

As for Shelagh, although perfectly well aware of her father's attitude on such matters, his extreme reaction and revulsion at her news was a little unexpected and she appeared almost shell-shocked. She pointed out that the Church, by its rigid rules on all-Catholic marriages, had left her little choice of a suitable partner, since Catholics were pretty thin on the ground in England. "I am nearly thirty-four" she insisted. "I've wasted twelve years. What hope have I got? Might as well have become a nun." Since she had not the slightest leaning in that direction the statement was entirely academic, but her arguments (as mine had) fell on deaf ears as far as Jack was concerned. In his eyes, she had transgressed against one of society's most sacred unwritten laws, and he never really forgave her.

Shortly before this, we had already decided to move again, having obtained permission to sub-let the Bolney Cottage, and returned to Hampshire. A relation of a friend of ours was turning a large house they owned at Fritham into two flats. I put in a bid for one and was successful. We left Sussex on a pouring wet day hoping to drive on ahead of the van in order to show the driver the way, but halfway there, we became stuck in the mud. Before we were able to extricate ourselves, the van passed us without noticing we were bogged down. When we finally arrived at Fritham, the van was there but there was no one to let us all in. The rain was still bucketing down when a neighbour finally turned up with the key and so, weather or not, unloading began. When all was done and just before its departure, the van, in manoeuvring its way out, pulled down an important-looking overhead cable. We fervently hoped it was telephone and not electricity. Fortunately it was, and it was repaired soon afterwards.

Snags in our tenure soon arose. The owner of the house and the friend with whom she shared the other flat treated us not as perfectly bona fide tenants, but as squatters. From the start, their very dictatorial manner made it clear that they rather resented sharing their house and that only financial considerations had forced them into this situation. They had no reason as far as we were concerned for this attitude. We were quiet, unassuming tenants, they saw little of us and we paid the rent regularly. But when we did meet, their frosty demeanour made it clear our presence was a necessary encumbrance.

A youth they employed to look after the garden was slightly mentally defective and had a disconcerting habit of exposing himself in front of our windows. That did not matter, and we could afford to ignore this behaviour when we were alone, but we could invite no one to come for a visit without risk of embarrassment. When I finally plucked up courage to broach the subject to our landlady she turned to her friend and remarked "Oh, he's at it again." We got no further on the subject and the situation continued as before. It was obvious that another move was in the offing, so a few months later, we rented a bungalow in Brockenhurst.

It is said that moving house is one of life's most stressful events, but I was one who positively thrived on it. Jack took little part in the preparations for moving and would retire to the quietest and emptiest room with a book while I got on with the packing. After we had been in the bungalow a few weeks, the people who owned it and a house nearby said they wished to sell both as one lot. We could have dug in our heels, refusing to quit an unfurnished property, as was our right, but I was delighted. Here was a ready-made excuse for moving and I did not even have to think of one!

Since I had a talent for winkling out rentable houses at crucial moments like these, we fixed on one near the the main Brockenhurst/Lymington road, nearly opposite the Balmer Lawn Hotel. It was a large Victorian house with three garages and an extensive rambling garden enclosing a well-maintained croquet lawn. Because of its size, the owner had been hard put to find tenants, as looking at it from the outside it would appear that a large staff would be required to run the place. Nothing daunted however, and congratulating ourselves on finding a house so conveniently close to the last, we took it on a short lease and moved in the following week.

The interior decorations left much to be desired and we spent quite a while cogitating over how much should be done and how much left undone to render the place habitable. The drawback was the number of rooms; I don't think we ever counted all the attics, which made improvements very expensive. It size was probably on a par with our old home at 29 Carlton Crescent but here, there was no one to help with the housework or cooking, and Jack was not fit enough to do more than a little gardening.

I was pleased as punch to find two of my old convent friends living just up the road. We had many a lively gossip recalling our youthful escapades and the many activities that made up our lives so long ago. On fine evenings Jack and I played croquet, that exasperating game in which, having got into a winning position, the opponent's ball comes flying over from some incredible angle and knocks one's own miles away again. We also went for walks through the Queen's Bower and very occasionally, for a spin in the car through the Rhododendron Drive towards Lyndhurst.

But with this renewed spate of rented accommodation, we longed for a home of our own again, particularly as our present lease was only a short one. I spent a considerable time visiting New Forest agents and poring over the property columns in the local newspapers and keeping a wary eye open for 'For Sale' notices on suitable houses when I went shopping. Before very long, we received particulars of a cottage outside Ringwood which was old but well-modernised. The owners had jobs in Bournemouth, which made commuting difficult. In view of this, they had decided to sell the house. It seemed ideal for us, with two downstairs rooms, an adequate kitchen, three bedrooms, a spacious bathroom upstairs, hot-air central heating and a small garden back and front with two good-sized sheds. It was on the old Salisbury Road and had extensive views over the River Avon as it wound its way through the green water meadows.

Cecil fixed us up with a bank loan for the cottage, an expensive transaction, but even then it was not easy to obtain mortgages on older properties. So when our last lease had come to an end and the sale had gone through, we moved in.

Cats are my favourite animals. In this latest house, I started a new venture breeding Blue Persians, using the warm, dry sheds for two expectant mothers (two sisters I had bought from a breeder friend). I named the mothers Minnie and Mercy after Minerva and Mercedes cars. None of the resulting kittens reached championship standard, but all were very pretty and fetched reasonable prices and I made sure they went to good, kind homes. Since there were always more would-be purchasers than kittens available, I was able to select who were to be the new owners, a satisfactory state of affairs for all concerned.

Our son Francis, who was now working for Norwich Union, came down on a summer holiday and drove me in our now rather elderly Morris to Goodwood for one of their last motor race meetings before the track was taken over. During the first race, a Formula I or II contest, the driver of a car described in the programme as 'The Sunset Special' was killed just as he was rounding that part of the circuit behind which we standing. He was thrown out of his car into the air by the fearful impact, falling back onto the grass beside the track, limp and loose-limbed like a discarded rag doll. It was a horrifying sight and after that day, I could never bring myself to watch the sport again live, although much later on, I did so on television when somehow, nothing seemed quite so real.

Jack and I enjoyed our little house at Ringwood. We were near enough to the library, shops and pub for him to be able to walk into the market town, choose his own books and have his pint of beer at the local. Many acquaintances used to gather there daily, and the landlord became quite a good friend of ours. Jack, an arch-hermit on most occasions, became quite sociable, especially when his particular pal, Hugh Hay Barclay, was present. They used to sit gossiping for what seemed like hours over a tankard, and often I had to dig him out of the lounge and ferry him home in the car for a late lunch.

There was quite a large Catholic church in Ringwood and when Francis came down, he and I joined the Legion of Mary, which met weekly at the presbytery to discuss various aspects of doctrine, arrange hospital visits and organise charity jumble sales or other fund-raising efforts. The former priest at the parish had been a dear old chap, at one time Aide de Camp to the Governor of India. He had also (even more importantly) been captain of the Hampshire Cricket Club! He had joined Beda College in Rome late in life, and Ringwood was either his first or nearly first parish. Age conquered him in the end and after a comparatively short time in office, he was forced to relinquish his duties to a younger man with whom unfortunately, we did not get on quite as well.

We had by now come to the conclusion that without sufficient capital, owning a house was too great a burden and too great a responsibility. Repairs and maintenance took too much of our spare income so once again, we sold up, barely recouping the money we had spent, but this time, we had no option. In short, we were completely broke, and could not keep up the repayments on interest or loan.

This time, it was Jack who found our new abode. He had some naval friends who had sold their house at Hightown outside Ringwood to someone who was still abroad and would be unable to take possession for a year. They were more than willing to let it during that period, to ensure that the house was kept warm and dry and the garden tended. Built about the beginning of the century, it was warm, attractive in layout and with spacious rooms rather too numerous for us, but the garden – oh dear! A grass path as wide as most lawns ran down to the woods 150 yards away. It boasted several springs, making mowing almost impossible. Under the trees and bushes that bordered this stretch of grass, the undergrowth was was lush and lank, requiring hours of intensive hard work to keep it even moderately tidy, but along one large flowerbed ran a hedge of yellow bush roses, the sweetest smelling I have ever come across. Even at some distance away, the scent was intoxicating.

Hightown was so isolated that a car was essential. Shelagh and her little boy, now aged three, came to stay with us for a week or two. Before the birth of the baby, she had married her Irishman, he having obtained a civil divorce, but the relationship had turned sour and they had separated soon after. It all seemed a rather sad and cynical waste of time. She and her father had now become partly reconciled, although they were never really comfortable in each other's presence, but Jack was very taken with his grandchild. "The lad utters strange oaths" he would remark, a twinkle in his eye, referring to the child's expressions such as "odds bodkins!" or "shiver me timbers!" gleaned from story books like *Treasure Island* or from comics. He really was the dearest little boy, as good as gold and surprisingly quiet for a three-year-old, and a friendly little fellow towards everyone. He had an enchanting way of earnestly answering "yes me do" or "me don't" in answer to a question. At this time, we had three other grandchildren, all boys, belonging to our eldest son John and were immensely proud of them.

On Boxing Day that year (1963), the weather turned very cold. A bitter east or north-east wind developed and hard on its heels came the snow. Day after day, there was no let-up. Snow, frost, more snow - and all the time, that piercing wind which nothing could keep out. The car remained in the garage for three months as we could not dig a path through the hard-packed snow to get it out of the gate. I would toil up the hill to the main road one and a half miles away to catch a bus into Ringwood. The baker stopped calling, the butcher, fishmonger and grocer followed suit. We were marooned.

Finally we ran out of coal and wood and the taxi refused to come up the lane so that we might fetch a bag of coal from the station. We were far from being the only sufferers in the district and flu became rampant during January and February, making matters worse if possible. The only thing that might be described as lucky where we were concerned was that neither of us fell ill during that gruelling time.

As had so often happened in the past, brother Cecil came to the rescue. Afraid that we would literally freeze to death, he came and collected us and took us to Lymington to live in the office flat until the bad weather was over. By this action I believe he saved our lives – perhaps not mine, as being still comparatively young and healthy, I could have survived, but certainly Jack's. While we were in Lymington, he told us that he would buy a small house or flat and let it to us as long as we wanted. He told us that the firm often purchased similar properties for their office staff and as we would be paying rent, we need feel under no obligation. Moreover, we could choose the house, bungalow or flat ourselves (within limits of course). Thus, with these encouraging words and with the car once more mobile, I began my now familiar job of househunting.

I tried Lymington first. It was readily accessible by bus and train to so many larger places and in addition, the ferry ran a shuttle service to the Isle of Wight and back during the summer months. We had only had two proper holidays in our long married life, neither of which we greatly enjoyed, and a day out to visit Yarmouth was an attractive prospect, especially as we both liked sleeping in our own beds at night. But for once, my searches proved abortive and Lymington yielded nothing suitable. Since neither Brockenhurst nor Ringwood had anything to offer either, I tried Lyndhurst and in a newly-developed conclave, I came upon some attractive maisonettes, some finished, some in the process of being built and each with its own garden plot. They had their own separate front doors and each had two bedrooms, large sitting room, kitchen and "coloured" bathroom (why that should be considered an asset I do not know) and separate lavatory, so Number Four, recently completed, became our new home.

Jack had never really been well since his retirement, and it was unfortunate that just before we moved, he was stricken with another attack of pneumonia. This may have been the result of our cold and miserable winter at Hightown. For a while he was in bad shape, but the antibiotics prevailed in the end and after a period of weakness he recovered and we settled down in Lyndhurst.

I suppose no one was surprised that before long, we discovered drawbacks. Lyndhurst, like most other New Forest villages, was dedicated to wooing the tourists, and in consequence, as well as many shortages, prices went up during the holiday season. Permanent residents hated the annual invasion and some of them fought tooth and nail with the Council against the annual encroachment. But it was all unavailing, and every year tourism increased.

The kitchen in our flat was cursed with a pale yellow and white tiled floor which I spent my life scrubbing, because every time anyone walked on it, it left marks. Why did I not notice this when we first looked over the flat? We had to carry coal up steep stairs from the bunker below. The tiny garden plot was well away from our maisonette and not worth having, as there was no privacy whatever. I cursed myself for not noticing these shortcomings, as they made everyday life uncomfortable. Shelagh and her little boy came down to stay for a while. She herself was managing to get by by obtaining jobs that included accommodation for them both such as school matron during term time and housekeeper during holiday periods.

After we had been in Lyndhurst for about a year, we moved again. We were now well into our sixties and on our beam ends! Francis had come down for a few days and suggested we join him in Norfolk and perhaps share a house with him. Although thirty-three years of age he had no particular girlfriends and was not at that time considering marrying anyone. We said we would give the matter some thought, but suggested he look around for a suitable house. The maisonettes at Lyndhurst had been selling like hot cakes during our first year at greatly-inflated prices, so we knew Cecil would have little difficulty in disposing of ours.

Barely a month later, Francis wrote to say he had found the very thing for us at a low rent and handy for his work in Norwich. It was a fairly new house in a place called Hethersett, a few miles south of Norwich. He met us on our arrival in Norfolk and told us that our current Blue Persian, Pippy, had arrived safely the previous evening but had so objected to the move that he had gone on hunger strike.

I was very impressed with Norwich, a beautiful city with its castle and lovely cathedral, but we could not forget that the house in Hethersett was on a short lease only, so a month later I phoned the Holt branch of Alfred Savill. To my astonishment, the young man who answered the phone immediately produced from his list two farmhouses to be let unfurnished on long leases at moderate rents. One was at Cley on the North Norfolk coast, the other at Trunch, further inland near Cromer, and as both sounded feasible, the following morning Francis got the day off work and hired a small car to take us to see them. The first, at Cley was too large, too cold and too far from Norwich, and as there were no suitable buses running in that direction, we turned it down.

The farmhouse at Trunch was a different proposition altogether. It was situated a few miles from North Walsham, from which both trains and buses ran frequently into the city. It was a charming place, well modernised and spacious with plenty of room for all of us, and even a guest or two should they want to pay us a visit. It belonged to a naval officer and the lease was for seven years. We thought that at last we had found a settled home.

The afternoon of our arrival, I was having a look round the garden before unpacking the vast amount of boxes and packages we had accumulated before coming to Norfolk when I came across a workman bending over a large concrete cover in the ground.

"What is that for?" I asked curiously.

"It's the well" came the reply.

"So you mean to say that, whilst we have main electricity there is only well-water available?" I asked. Shades of Halifax! Apart from Halifax, we had never been reduced to a well for all our extensive needs of drinking, washing, cooking, baths etc.

"Don't worry," he said. "It has never been known to run dry and the pressure is good. I don't think you will notice the difference and the water is soft and pure." And he was right.

At the time, I was a bit unnerved by this discovery, but Jack and Francis were not prepared to share my worries. They told me not to fuss but to get on with the business of sorting out our things, as they were both anxious to see if all their gadgets were safe and sound and unharmed by the removal. One of Jack's hobbies was the construction of model sailing ships with very delicate parts, while Francis had accumulated valuable books and musical instruments such as recorders and flutes.

We settled down easily in that farmhouse. Pippy loved the garden. In addition to her, we had more or less inherited a farm cat left behind by the last people who had lived there before the house had been enlarged and modernised. The tortoiseshell cat, whom we named Mother, was very wild, heavily pregnant and terribly hungry, avidly scoffing the crumbs of cake and bread we put out for the birds, so I put down some suitable food for her too, which she wolfed down quietly when the garden was empty of humans or other animals.

She went missing for several weeks, until one day when Jack and I were looking over the old stables I perceived a slight movement below a crumbling wall. At first I took it to be rats, but on approaching cautiously, I saw three beautiful half-Persian kittens crouching on the dirty ground. When we tiptoed in to pick them up, we noticed that they were ginger, grey and a pale cream respectively. They had pretty faces and big round eyes.

But once in our hands, we found ourselves clutching three screaming furies. They scratched and bit and with ears flat against their heads, struggled desperately to get free. They were no bigger than rats and once put down, rodent-like they scurried hastily through a hole in the wall.

Some time after this encounter, Mother brought her kittens over one by one to join in her meals. They could then run around by themselves, but solicitous as ever for their welfare, she kept her eyes and ears open for the slightest indication of danger and after the meal, would usher them under a gate into a field opposite, where presumably, the family lived. When they were about six months old, the kittens let me pick them up and give them milk in a saucer. Mother was then expecting again, so I advertised the grey female and found her a good home. The two males, Ginger and Scruffy, we kept as pets.

The second lot of kittens born in the garden under a tree were in imminent danger of being mown down by Francis when he scythed the long grass, so I settled the whole family in a shed. Mother was quite friendly by this time and although allowing me to handle her babies and even purring when I held them, she would never let me touch her or stroke her, holding up an admonitory paw whenever I showed signs of getting too close for her liking. In due course I advertised and found homes for the second lot, but as it was impossible to catch the mother to have her spayed, I decided most reluctantly to have her put to sleep, as it would not be possible to place all the unlimited production line and I could not leave them to starve.

The day before the RSPCA official was due to come and fetch her, Francis and I went for a long walk. Although such a thing had never happened before, Mother joined us and stayed beside us for the whole of that afternoon. Every few yards, she would run ahead, then turn and wait for us to catch her up, miaowing in a peculiar sort of pleading manner. The walk was a long one of a few miles, but she came every step of the way there and back, never leaving us once. There seemed no explanation for this unprecedented behaviour on her part. Did she somehow have a premonition of her impending fate? Poor Mother. I have never got over the feeling of guilt and betrayal for having planned her untimely death, and we missed her greatly for some time afterwards.

We lost poor Pippy also. At only eight years old, she inexplicably developed cancer of the liver, and although undoubtedly in pain and eventually also having to be put down, she was not once sick or dirty and even when jaundice became established and she could no longer eat, she still purred whenever I spoke to her or stroked her bony back. AG Street once said "if you have livestock, sooner or later, you will have deadstock on your hands." Well, he was a farmer with probably not quite the same sentimental attitude as ours, but it is a sad fact that an animal's lifespan is generally shorter than our own and it is still heartbreaking to lose a beloved pet.

Our previous car had been disposed of before we came to Norfolk but situated as we were, one was badly needed, so we bought another Morris Minor for £25. Everything seemed to be going smoothly and for eighteen months we were very happy in our Trunch home. Francis then announced that he had met a girl he wanted to marry and they would be moving into her own little cottage after the ceremony. Naturally, we were delighted at his news, but realised that here was another move coming up. In any case, the house was far too large for just the two of us.

Shelagh had recently remarried. Her husband was a Norfolk man who owned a house in Trimingham and some holiday flats in Cromer, where they were then living. He agreed to let us live in the Trimingham house for the time being at a modest rent, a kindness which made all the difference to our rather depressed outlook at the time.

We had not been installed in this new abode for very long when Jack fell ill again with one of his usual attacks of pneumonia. This time his breathing was difficult, and he found going up and down stairs so tiring that our doctor sent him to see a heart specialist in Cromer. Immediate admission into hospital was advised, together with complete rest in bed.

After the first week, he started to improve and at last seemed on his way to a full recovery. We then went to stay with my brother Mervyn in Surrey, a change we felt would do him good. Mervyn's daughter Gillian drove all the way from London to fetch us and take us back to Surrey on the same day, a marathon journey! We stayed there a month and by the end of the visit, Jack was himself again, sleeping and eating well. Mervyn drove us back to Trimingham, but our days there were rapidly coming to a close. Shelagh's husband was paying a heavy mortgage on their house in Cromer and another on the Trimingham place. With only a modest salary, he obviously could not keep up both for long, but he took no steps to speed our departure and kindly accepted the fact that it might be some time before he could get possession and sell the second place.

Then our other son, John, came to the rescue. "Don't make any permanent arrangement about houses in Norfolk" he said. "If we can get a suitable place, say between London and Portsmouth, we would like you both to come and share with us." This was heaven-sent. I got in touch with Savill's again and this time, wrote to their Wimborne office asking if they by any chance had on their books a house with at least six bedrooms, two bathrooms and two kitchens. John and Constance ('Bunny'), his wife, now had five children, all boys. We needed all the space we could get.

"Nothing of that description between London and Portsmouth," came the prompt reply. "But there is such a property coming on our books outside Lyme Regis in

Dorset which I am sure would suit you. The rent (here he quoted an estimated reasonable figure) is at the moment being assessed and as soon as this has been settled, I will send you full particulars."

A month went by with no further word and just as we had given up hope, a letter came from the Wimborne office with full particulars of a lovely old modernised farmhouse with just the accommodation we needed, two and a half miles from Lyme Regis. John, now in the Navy, was away on HMS *Bulwark* and I forwarded the letter and particulars to his wife for her approval, asking if she would go and view, as it was too far away for us to do so. Bunny, who was a great character, did so, and declared afterwards, "Well, I can't help it if no one else likes it, but I like it!" which of course settled matters. She well knew that we would all love it.

I had been on tenterhooks until the evening of my daughter-in-law's scheduled visit to Dorset and walked restlessly up and down the room waiting impatiently for the expected phone call. We had now geared ourselves fully for departure from Norfolk. I felt sure Jack would be unable to withstand another winter on the North Norfolk coast, beautiful as it was, and hoped fervently his health might improve in a kinder more southern clime.

"It is a beautiful spot" said Bunny when she phoned. "Shall I take it?"

"Take it" I urged. "It sounds perfect. We'll never get anything else as good."

Jack, having read through the particulars carefully, had already made his decision that it was just the place for us.

We said goodbye excitedly and I replaced the receiver with a relieved sigh. Were things at last looking up? We were now too old to continue leading so nomadic an existence and Jack, a little older than I, was in too poor a state of health to continue being uprooted. It was now becoming urgent to have somewhere permanent to lay our heads. Jack, while very much liking the sound of our prospective new home, dreaded the idea of the long journey with all our belongings, furniture, three cats (one extra now), not to mention having to change doctors, which he liked least of all. There was little I could say or do to console him on this score, but I promised to do all the spadework, the packing and all the details of the move. I would ask Francis to meet us at Norwich Station and help us across the platform with our luggage and livestock and get Mervyn to meet us at Liverpool Street Station and take us to his place for the night. Finally, Shelagh promised to tidy the cottage on our departure, so we would not have to bother about any mess left behind. Thus I hoped to lessen his anxiety about the projected upheaval.

A fortnight passed. Then, we heard the lease would be dated from May 5th and so plans were put into operation for that day – a Tuesday. We decided to go down on the Monday, stay one night at a hotel in Lyme Regis and go to the house early the next morning to be ready for the carrier when he arrived with our things. This meant scrapping the proposed visit to Mervyn, but we reckoned if he could just help us across London with all the gear, we could have a night or two later with him to recuperate.

CHAPTER THIRTEEN

FINALLY AT REST

When the great day dawned, everything went according to plan and Jack seemed not nearly as exhausted as I had expected. We were met by a good friend of mine, Milly, at Sherborne. She took the cat baskets from us in order to put the three of them in kennels for a week, to enable us to get straightened out in the meantime. She had already booked us into a hotel. The carrier from Norfolk reckoned he should arrive at the house any time after ten o'clock in the morning, so we collected a picnic lunch from our overnight hotel and made our way to the house to meet the van.

Everything seemed to be going smoothly. The previous tenant had left Dunlopillo window seat cushions, so we were able to sit comfortably looking out at the charming garden. Between the trees at the end of the lawn a the glimpse of a sparkling blue sea – ('*es lachelt der see, er ladet zum baden*') – no, not warm enough for bathing, but it did look most enticing.

We waited all that morning, periodically going to the front door to scan the long drive, but nothing and no one came. Bunny arrived in a taxi about 2 pm and shortly afterwards Pickford's came with her furniture, but still no sign of our carrier George. All that sunny afternoon, we lazed uneasily on Bunny's chairs but could not settle.

At 7 pm I telephoned Mrs C, George's wife. "He left last night" she replied, understandably agitated by my enquiry. "He expected to be with you no later than two o'clock. I can't think what could have gone wrong. He knew the route well enough and the van has only just been tested and overhauled."

It was now beginning to get dark and at 10 pm I contacted the police at Axminster to ask if any lorries had reported a breakdown or been involved in an accident, but drew a blank. By 11.30, Jack and I had practically resigned ourselves to never seeing our things again, but as a last throw of the dice I walked slowly along the main road to the Axminster turning. I caught sight of a tall dark shape about to emerge, but it had crossed the road before I could get near and quickly disappeared down the lane on the opposite side, a cul-de-sac. The driver must have mistaken the turning, I thought. Within a few minutes, as I waited to see what would happen, the van reappeared and George's head and shoulders leaned wearily from the cab. "What a time I've had getting here. First, I got a puncture, then I found the return load we were supposed to pick up would not be ready in time and then I lost the way."

"Never mind" I said, feeling almost lightheaded with relief. "We'll all help you unload. I'll get you some supper and we'll fix you up with a bed for the night."

"I'll sleep on some blankets in the van," George said. "Then I'll be off at first light without disturbing anybody."

In spite of all our care when unloading to make as little noise as possible at that time in the still country night, dogs near and far began to bark. I saw lights switched on and knew guiltily that we had probably disturbed the entire neighbourhood. It was after 1 am by the time everything was off the van.

Bunny and I had a wonderful time during the first six months going to auction sales. At that time, things were not as dear, nor were there as many dealers, and we gradually acquired sufficient furniture and carpets to give the house a homely and lived-in appearance and to get the necessary garden tools and equipment.

John came home in October. He too was delighted with our beautiful new home and set to work to put up shelves, repair tables and chairs, render all electrical gadgets foolproof and safe, and mend every clock on the premises. By the time this ultra-efficient handyman had finished, everything in the house was in perfect working order. John had always had the sort of mind that viewed all machinery in simple mathematical terms, everything in its right place and doing its job and if not, he wanted to know why and usually did. Unfortunately, his next naval appointment was again abroad and during his absence, we sorely missed his expertise.

Our first Christmas dinner in our new home was enjoyed in the spacious dining room surrounded by children, presents everywhere, a mound of paper wrappings and quite a drop to drink! Shopping was now infinitely easier. I had bought a second-hand Morris Minor from Mervyn's daughter and now even a moderate social life could be indulged in, so once more, I played bridge and joined the WI and the British Legion, and Bunny took up singing with the local operatic society.

Jack passed his days in his bright and warm bedroom looking across the garden to a view of the sea where he had spent so much of his younger life and which had once been his great love. When he felt up to it, he could indulge his hobbies of ship-modelling, oil painting and most of all, reading. He had always been a voracious reader and I had a hard time in the local library sifting out books he had read from those he wanted to read and the ones he would not even look at.

During our second winter in Dorset, another attack of pneumonia struck him down. Before he was over the illness, our own well-beloved doctor was himself suddenly taken ill and died in Axminster Hospital. After this tragedy, the district was served by a series of locums. The consequence was that Jack failed to get his usual X-ray after his illness had subsided. We well knew by then that his lungs were in a very serious condition. He had long ago given up smoking but it was probably too late. By the end of March, his illness was dragging on well beyond the usual time of recovery. Some days seemed to bring an improvement in his condition and on those brighter mornings, my hopes rose a little, but it was only temporary, and the following day I would feel despair at the sight of his unutterably tired eyes.

In April, a small lump made its appearance in the groin. I called the doctor immediately. "Only a sebacious cyst" was his confident verdict. "Nothing at all to worry about, but should it become in any way troublesome, it can easily be removed later in the summer when the weather is warmer." I was so relieved by this diagnosis, and the sun outside seemed to shine all the brighter for the news. Jack did not appear quite so elated. There were strange shadows on his face as he got back into bed and lay down. "I hope to God he's right," was all he said.

As time progressed, the lump grew larger and a deep

red mark began to show around the area. While we were still assured it was in all probability merely a cyst, an appointment was made to see someone in hospital about having it removed. Jack was now up and about again and usually joined us at lunch but his breathlessness was such that he could manage only four of the shallow stairs at a time, and needed a stick to walk slowly round the garden. The breathlessness manifested itself so badly when at the hospital that the surgeon was reluctant to operate and I was told to bring him back in a month's time.

On our second visit, the surgeon was definitely disturbed by the appearance of the 'cyst' and ordered an immediate biopsy. Our worst fears were confirmed when the results came through ten days later and an appointment was made for him to go into Exeter Hospital for a complete examination. During the waiting period he looked and felt very ill, slept little and had no appetite. As his weight dropped rapidly my hopes for his recovery gradually faded, but I took care not to let him see how desperately worried I was.

But all this tension finally broke my self-control one awful day. After trying everything I could think of to get him to take some nourishment and finding the meal untouched when I came to remove the tray, I threw the dishes on the floor and smashed the lot, the pieces lying all over the carpet mixed up with fragments of food. Jack wept at my action and protested that he was too ill to eat. I was wretched beyond measure at what I had done, but the worry, the sleepless nights and above all, the constant raising and dashing of hopes proved too much on that occasion. "If only we knew what to do!" I cried, and wept with him. "If only there was someone to turn to for help."

Two days before he was due to go into hospital he lost his voice. "Laryngitis" was the doctor's verdict. "But how could I have caught it?" he whispered. "I haven't been out and no one with a cold has been anywhere near me." However, because of possible infection, the hospital appointment was cancelled and we were told another would be made as soon as his voice returned to normal.

For three weeks we hoped and prayed this would right itself sufficiently to allow him to keep his postponed appointment, but although very occasionally, a few words would issue from his lips in something like his usual tones, by nightfall, when he was tired, his voice had faded once more and only the merest whisper came in answer to my anxious enquiry. Poor Jack, my long-suffering husband. It was truly agonising to see his remaining strength fading, his lungs aching. Now that his voice had gone, I felt that unless he could be speedily got into hospital, there was no hope for him at all.

On June 7th, the doctor ordered an ambulance to take him to Exeter that same afternoon. I rang in the evening to ask the sister if he had settled down. "Oh yes" she answered, "but has he any trouble with his sight? He seems to find it difficult to read the time by his watch and says the light in his room is bad."

Bunny rang the following morning when I was getting ready to visit him at the hospital. "Ah, but he's a very sick man" were Sister's alarming words. "He has just had an X-ray and although it may be possible to deal with the trouble in the groin, it is his lungs we are so worried about. They are full of cancer." With these words, I knew there was no hope left. He died a short time afterwards.

On those early summer evenings, I sat at his window looking out at the view he had got to know so well in those past few months. A star shone overhead, the pine tree stood sentinel at the end of the lawn, black against the darkening sky and a shaft of moonlight beamed over our small glimpse of sea. As I sat there meditating on our long married life together, I recalled Jack's words written from China so many years before when we were also apart and missed each other so much: "When I look at the path of the moonlight over the sea, I comfort myself that it is really only a little way I have to travel to find you again."

It is only a little way, my darling. As time passes, it grows ever less, until one day, the beginning and the end will merge and we will once more be together.

Printed in Great Britain
by Amazon.co.uk, Ltd.,
Marston Gate.